# WINNING WATERS

# WINNING

# WATERS

*The Homes of Rowing*

WRITTEN AND ILLUSTRATED BY
*Aylwin Sampson*

*Foreword by HRH Prince Michael of Kent*

ROBERT HALE · LONDON

*By the same author*
Somerset Scenes
Grounds of Appeal: The Homes of First-Class Cricket
Courses of Action: The Homes of Horse Racing

© *Aylwin Sampson 1986*
*First published in Great Britain 1986*

ISBN 0 7090 2722 2

Robert Hale Limited
Clerkenwell House
Clerkenwell Green
London EC1R 0HT

British Library Cataloguing in Publication Data

Sampson, Aylwin
    Winning waters: the homes of rowing.
    1. Rowing—Great Britain—Handbooks,
    manuals, etc.
    I. Title
791.1'23'0941

ISBN 0-7090-2722-2

Photoset in North Wales by
Derek Doyle & Associates, Mold, Clwyd.
Printed in Great Britain by
Redwood Burn Ltd., Trowbridge, Wiltshire.
Bound by WBC Bookbinders Limited.

# Foreword by
# HRH Prince Michael of Kent

I WAS VERY pleased to be asked to write a foreword to this book, because I look back exactly a quarter of a century to the year I used to be an oar myself – one of the most enjoyable summers I can remember.

My first experience in a boat was sculling, a career begun inauspiciously at Eton, when this idle wet-bob was given the slowest and heaviest whiff out of Rafts. The problem with sculling is that if you have one arm stronger than the other, you tend to go round in circles. This is what happened to me, and I never graduated to a rigger till the age of eighteen. I was definitely not cut out for sculling.

After Eton I found myself at the Royal Military Academy, Sandhurst, where the standard of physical fitness for all us officer cadets was inordinately high. I was asked if I would like to row for the Academy and at once accepted. The chief reason (and I kept it to myself) was that, no matter what sin you had committed on the parade ground that morning so that the authorities confined you to barracks as a result, the one loophole in the military law as it stood was that, provided that when you did a sport you did it representing the Academy, you were allowed out beyond the grounds. I had made it my business to grasp the niceties of that law at an early stage.

In the summer of 1961, I rowed in the Sandhurst coxed four. We kept it at the Reading University Boat Club boathouse and took it out two or three afternoons a week. We competed at several regattas that season. At Pangbourne, on the hottest day of the year in June, we got through to the finals, winning two of the heats by less than a canvas. I well remember the agony when we were ourselves beaten by a canvas in the final race. We also went to Stratford-upon-Avon and Wallingford and fared indifferently.

The most unfortunate episode occurred when we were invited to take part in the Reading Working Men's Regatta, in one of their boats. On the command: 'Are you ready? Row!', I took a powerful three-quarter stroke, whereupon the rigger came clean away from the side of the boat, and we were left sitting forlornly in our dismembered vessel and not allowed, needless to say, to restart.

Glory came at the last competition of the season, Bedford Amateur Regatta. We reached the quarter-finals, to our great surprise. Never thinking we would be likely to progress to the semi-finals, we began to drown our end-of-season sorrows in champagne. But we did win the semi-finals. Certain, now, that we had really reached our limits (and hoping it, too, because some of us had arranged to take ladies to the theatre in London), we commandeered yet more champagne. Stroke even drew deeply on a cigar, I remember. However, I do not recall very much about the last race, except groans and coughing and the discomfort of rowing on a stomachful of bubbles. But luck was on our side, because our hapless opponents managed to steer into us; our oars were fouled; and the Maiden Fours Cup was ours. Ignominious perhaps, but still victory.

Rowing today is possible taken more seriously than that. I do hope not, because when sport gets too serious, it always changes for the worse and sportsmanship only stands to suffer.

I have immensely enjoyed reading *Winning Waters* and looking at its excellent and nostalgic drawings. I know you will too.

# Contents

## List of Illustrations

# *Preface*

THIS BOOK, like its two earlier companion volumes, is principally concerned with the environment of a sport. Inevitably reference must be made to club history and successes but, to adapt the term used by HRH Prince Philip in his Foreword to my first book, about cricket grounds, the emphasis is on 'greater rowing'.

Here I have tried to convey through drawings as well as words something of the rich variety and wide-ranging character of setting, the complex pattern of clubs' development and, above all, the fascination regatta or Head can have for rower and spectator alike.

In this attempt I have been immeasurably helped by the enthusiasm of secretaries, members and rowing people throughout the country, while the Amateur Rowing Association has been invaluable in 'smoothing my path'. To them all thanks are due, and I am greatly appreciative of the interest shown by HRH Prince Michael of Kent in his Foreword.

*A.A.S.*
*Cheltenham*

**Inset (top right):**

Oxford
Radley
Abingdon
Marlow
Maidenhead
Wallingford
Brentford
Chiswick
Henley
Pangbourne
Reading
Eton
Poplar
Greenwich
Laleham
Weybridge
Gravesend
Putney
Kingston
Hammersmith
Twickenham

**Main map:**

Loch Lomond
Clyde
GLASGOW
Nithsdale
Talkin Tarn
Tyne
Durham
Whitby
Lancaster
York
Bradford
Hollingworth Lake
Liverpool
Salford
Birkenhead
Chester
Derby
Nottingham
Burton
Shrewsbury
Norwich
Ironbridge
Peterborough
Bewdley
BIRMINGHAM
Stourport
St.Ives
Ely
Worcester
Stratford
St.Neots
Cambridge
Hereford
Evesham
Bedford
Sudbury
Ross
Tewkesbury
Gloucester
SEE INSET ABOVE
Penarth
Bristol
Rochester
Chatham
Bradford-on-Avon
Folkestone
Dover
Bideford
Southampton
Blandford
Southsea
Ryde
Christchurch
Fowey
Dartmouth
Falmouth

Miles
0        50

0        50
km

# Introduction

IT COULD BE said that sports are of two kinds: those owing their origin to the necessities of existence, where the primary purposes of getting food or fighting for survival have been transformed into recognizable imitations, and those which have been invented purely for recreation, with their competition, their elaborate rules and indeed their artificialities.

Rowing does not fall easily into either of these categories, for on the one hand its origins undoubtedly are rooted in necessity, while on the other the simplicity of the sport almost removes it from the company of other games.

Where rowing can claim some kind of uniqueness is in its setting. The so-called field sports demand the culture of a quarry; games require the provision of a more or less contrived environment. But rowing uses what it is given; water cannot be contoured, mown or modified. Admittedly there will have been a choice, yet it is noteworthy how frequently clubs declare the unsuitability of their courses. For the challenge is not only between crews but also with the element.

How right that this should be so. There may be a powerful case for uniformity of direction, distance and demands in the stopwatch world of Olympics and International Championships. Indeed, it is undeniable that there are basic requirements: space to row and turn around; a width of at least twenty-six feet (eight metres) to include the sweep of the oars, more like thirty-eight feet (twelve metres) if steering is allowed for, adding up to seventy-seven feet (twenty-four metres) width for side-by-side racing. So far as length is concerned, the ideal minimum would be 3,000 feet (1,000 metres), to enable some five minutes of rowing, while the experienced would like four-six mile (eight- to ten-kilometre) outings. Yet surely the awkward bend, the narrow bridge or the coastal current give that individuality which can be called character. Do golf courses standardize their holes, or racecourses iron out their gradients?

No, it is in the variety of challenge that the skill rejoices; sport is not measured by minimizing the range of mastery. Is not another name for all this 'craft'?

Take away the individuality of the setting, and the spectator too will be the poorer. Waters are in a context too: one may be in the pastoral charm of wooded valley, another may be found amongst a city's commerce; others are in estuary, lake, coast, country park or reservoir.

For the majority of regattas it will be a moderately straight stretch of river, where no staggering of start or finish is needed to ensure fairness to all competitors. The problems of crosswinds may well decide on the exact positions of the racing lanes, and it frequently means that there are buoys, maybe only plastic cans, acting as markers. Most courses on rivers have but two lanes, necessitating a large number of heats. A recommendation has been made that no more than sixteen entries be accepted, to reduce the preliminary races to a reasonable maximum. Where there are waters allowing multi-lane rowing, as for example on reservoirs or at the purpose-built water-sports centres of Holme Pierrepont and Strathclyde Loch, then another procedure can be employed, namely 'repêchage'. This term meaning literally 'second chance', offers the losing crews in the heats an opportunity to compete for a place in the finals by racing against each other. Clearly such a system will work best in the six-lane courses to be found in those generously endowed waters.

In the case of Head of the River, or processional, races the situation is somewhat different. In theory these could be held in a single-lane stretch of water, and indeed the bumping races at Cambridge, for example, developed because of the narrowness of

2

the Cam. However, in practice there is normally room for at least two crews side by side even though the principle is not that one should pass the other. These races are basically against the clock, each boat starting individually and striving to arrive at the finish in the fastest time. Inevitably there is not the immediate drama of a close-fought contest with the visual excitement of a University boat race or Henley final, yet there is another kind of tension. Perhaps it is something to do with the demands of invisible competitors, the unseen pressure. Certainly every crew that rows in these races exhibits as much energy as, sometimes more concern than, a losing boat at a regatta race. Further, there is unquestionably a stirring grandeur, even majesty, about the marshalling area before the start of a large Head. The inexorable filing of boats making their way upstream, for normally all racing is downstream, quietly conserving every muscle, has almost the quality of a pre-battle march or a backstage assembly before the curtain rises. And of course the drama overall lasts often four times as long as a regatta race, for the distances are much longer. But whether regatta or Head of the River, the boats will be the same, unless of course it is coastal rowing, when a more robust craft is needed. The largest racing boat, or shell as it is called, is the eight. With a length of up to 62 feet (18.9 metres) but weighing only 250 pounds, it presents, at full speed, an experience both memorable and stirring for rower and spectator. Its development owed much to the public schools and universities, for here was a relatively economic use of those wishing to row. It is today debatable if that economy extends to cost, £5-6,000 being a normal figure to pay. Arrangements of oar positions have varied, but traditionally the rower nearest the cox has the port side, the remaining members of the crew alternating. A further variation has been the moving of the cox to the bow, for reasons of visibility and wind resistance chiefly.

The other types of crew make-up extend through coxed and coxless fours, coxed and coxless pairs, while the distinction has then to be made with sculling, where two oars, or blades as they are termed, are used by each person. The variations here are fewer, being double or single.

Such then are the craft, but there is still much to understand in the matter of handling them. With fragile and valuable possessions like

3

these, any club will ensure that they are handled competently. This is where the duties of the cox begin. Getting a boat to the water is itself a disciplined matter, beginning with unloading it from the trailer or boathouse rack. To observe the smooth teamwork necessary as the crew carry the upside-down shell to the raft or bank steps, pointing the bow upstream, then at the command turning it right-way up, with half the crew going underneath it to be on the land side, is in itself an instructive sight at every regatta. Add to this the various crisp orders given by the cox, in terms standardized over many years, such terms as 'easy all' meaning 'stop rowing', 'spin her' meaning turning the boat by one side rowing normally, the other reversing the stroke, and 'back stops' meaning taking up a position of having completed one stroke, and awaiting instructions.

It has already been stated that rowing is an uncomplicated pastime, and indeed competitive rowing is very much less elaborate than any other contest sport, but a regatta has to have some rules, however simple. The start of a race, usually upstream and possibly out of sight of the judges and spectators at the finish, may be either

At Durham the regatta course on the River Wear enjoys one of the finest panoramas to be seen anywhere in the country. Between the new Elvet Bridge which carries the much-needed bypass round the city, and its twelfth-century namesake the first of the course's challenging curves begins. The cutwaters of old Elvet Bridge bear numbers to show the coxed fours that no. 1 is 'easy arch' and No. 2 'hard', where there is little clearance for blades. On the right-hand bank, in the illustration, Brown's boathouse provides an excellent grandstand for the spectators; it has occupied this site since 1826, and for over a century racing boats have been built here. It is here also that the short course finishes.

The long course continues through the bridge to Bow Corner and Minute Tree Reach, so called to indicate how much longer the crews can expect to labour.

In the drawing it is not possible to show all of the nine arches which Elvet Bridge has, despite a destructive flood in 1771, and the two chapels formerly there have unfortunately gone, but the dominating castle and cathedral, those 'mixed and massive piles' beloved by Sir Walter Scott, still provide a backcloth to this impressive scene.

from stake boats or free. It is signalled by the raising of a flag followed by the question from the official 'Are you ready?' and then 'Go'. Such simplicity is continued through the race, the only proviso being that there must be no interference by one crew with another, either by encroaching on a competitor's station, or lane, or by physical contact of boat, blade or person. (Here, it may be added, such niceties have not always obtained, for it was common practice in the early years of competitive rowing to engage in these unsporting tactics.) Along the course there will be officials to ensure that fair use of the water continues, though in one or two instances, as at Henley and the University Boat Race, the umpire will follow in a launch.

So then to the finish and, at the end of the regatta, those important presentations of prizes and mementos: tankards, medals or pennants.

One other source of mystery to the spectator may be found in the multitude of designations given to crews. There are six categories for competitors, based partly on age, partly on performance or even on weight. The first term is that of junior, signifying that the rower, or smaller, is under eighteen years – or, to be exact, was not that age on the first day of the current year. There are subdivisions of this classification, namely under sixteen, under fifteen and under fourteen, though for all these the qualifying date is 1 September of the previous year. A senior will have been eighteen years on 1 January. However, if that person has won six qualifying events anytime and goes on to add another four in that year, or indeed has competed in an Olympic or World Championship, the classification changes to 'élite'. A 'veteran' has reached the age of twenty-seven; a 'novice' will not have won an open event at a regatta, and a 'lightweight' will weigh less than 160 pounds (72.5 kilograms).

Here then are some of the facets of regatta rowing. Obviously Head of the River racing, coastal rowing and skiff racing as well as such regional variations as Cornish rowing will have their individual rules.

In passing it should be mentioned that there is also what has been termed social rowing; here the non-competitive element predominates, and the alternative descriptions such as touring

6

rowing or leisure rowing – and sculling can well be substituted for all these – are indications not only of their characters but also of the fact that Jerome K. Jerome's *Three Men in a Boat* is being reborn.

Just as courses vary, so do boathouses. The once common Victorian or Edwardian style with its elaborate wooden balcony, its half-timbered gable and its air of leisured comfort is rapidly disappearing, while the rudimentary shed, of corrugated iron or asbestos panelling, also gives place to the modern, somewhat characterless structure of concrete and cladding. Fortunately there are those which, through a sensitive use of crisply painted detailing, preserve the quality of waterside architecture.

Sometimes clubhouse and boatstore are separate, usually with the latter very much a second-best. Or there may be just a tubular steel and canvas shelter nearby to serve the purpose. Obviously any boatstore must be planned around the boat size: a four, for example, requires at least forty-five feet (fourteen metres) length and six feet (two metres) width with movement space as well.

Normally the finish of a regatta course will be at or near the clubhouse, where activity both on and off the water is at its height: shells being unloaded from trailers, crews making adjustments to riggers or seats, blades everywhere, and spectators deftly dodging them all!

There are visual and aural features on the water too. Colour confines itself to the oars and rowing vests. In the past there would have been somewhat more extravagance: the 1793 Oxford University college crews wore straw hats, sashes, even tam o'shanters with chequered bands in the case of Christ Church in 1819. Durham University oarsmen in the 1830s were required to wear an academical cap or boating cap on the river, and on the way to the boathouse cap and gown. Henley crews in 1839 boasted blue caps, gold tassels, striped jerseys and rosettes. And of course, for Doggetts Coat and Badge race, begun in 1715, the contestants would have normally worn the livery of their employers, or a silk hat.

Since the introduction of sliding seats in 1871, the rhythm of rowing, for the spectator at least, has been changed. Now there is a strange illusion, seen particularly with coxed crews, where the boat appears to accelerate forward in spurts. Added to this, the sound of the slide can also be heard, as if the boat, or crew, suffers from asthma.

Of rowing history, technical and social, much has already been written, Enough here to outline some facets.

The nineteenth-century increase in leisure time combined with the public school ethos of athleticism produced a new era in rowing. Before this time professional watermen had been the focus of vicarious sport, being the subjects of wagers on their races. With the peace that followed the end of the Napoleonic Wars, pleasure boating and public school rowing expanded. Railway transport was available for the boats themselves, and consequently it was possible for the rapidly proliferating clubs to travel around the regattas. Such events owed their inception to the popularity of the eighteenth-century Processions of Boats: in 1768 Walton-on-Thames 'regatta' was reported by William Hickey, and in 1775 Ranelagh's attracted over 200,000 spectators, albeit lured by the gaming booths.

Membership of these clubs founded in the 1860s and 70s was largely middle-class, but it is interesting to note that, until the formation of the ARA in 1882, the participation of artisan and professional waterman was accepted. The segregation after this date was exacerbated in 1890 by the founding of the NARA, and it was not until 1956 that the last vestiges of class or occupational distinction disappeared. By the 1880s and 90s the growth in club membership fell off, perhaps due to the ascending popularity of tennis, cycling and golf. Nevertheless, despite the relative costliness of rowing in time, convenience and equipment, there has never been wanting a succession of rowers, willing to subscribe to their club and prepared to put in hours of training.

Today these clubs, whether claiming local allegiance or 'closed' membership from business, school, university and college, may all call themselves amateur – and that must mean a 'lover of the sport' as well.

This then is rowing, one of the few remaining sports that has a wide spectrum of appeal; it is accorded an élitist image conjured up when Henley is mentioned, yet all levels of the community practise it. As a team sport there is no other that can surpass its ideal of perfect synchronization and unison, as exemplified in the racing eight. It is a highly physical, non-contact, whole-body sport requiring a balanced overall training, developing stamina and strength. But above all it is a clean sport, virtually free from drug-taking and financial 'back-handers', and mercifully without the cult of 'personality'.

As Steve Fairbairn, that oarsman who did so much for the sport, put it: 'The whole sensation is one of joy and exhilaration.'

# CHAPTER ONE

## *North*

### DURHAM · TALKIN TARN · TYNE

IF A HOME of rowing is created by a combination of history, tradition and setting, Durham may fairly claim to be, in the motto of Hatfield College, if not the first, then amongst the first. For here are to be found a magnificently sited castle, a cathedral of major importance in European architecture, a city complementing the superb group on its rock, a university exceeded in England only by Oxford and Cambridge in age, and a river which acts as a cord binding all together.

Without doubt it is chiefly owing to the university and Durham School that here the centre of rowing in northern England has developed. The sport was taken up enthusiastically from the very first days of the university, and the fact that top hats were worn even at the oar was not a deterrent. From 1815 the celebrating of Waterloo found expression in a Procession of Boats; in 1834, five years before Henley, the university was instrumental in establishing the regatta, and a university boat race between Durham and Edinburgh began in 1904. All this on a river that was not wide enough for eights, with a bridge and bends that would tax the most experienced of crews.

For here at Durham are two of the oldest rowing clubs in the country, and one of the oldest regattas; today nineteen clubs from twelve boathouses use this two-mile stretch of the River Wear through to the very centre of the city. The navigable water starts upstream at Shincliffe Bridge, but bends, narrowness and occasional

At the end of Minute Tree Reach, the long course on the Wear at Durham has its finish marked by the garden wall of the Count's House. This Greek Revival temple of about 1820 was in fact the summerhouse of a Polish dwarf named Count Borluwlaski.

A little further downstream, Prebends' Bridge, built by George Nicholson in 1777, provides a view of the last group of boathouses on this Durham water. On the left side of the drawing is Durham School boathouse, next to the old cornmill, today the Durham Canoe Club headquarters; on the other side of the Pool, across the weir, or Stakes as it is called, the fulling-mill, now the university archaeology museum, has as its neighbours the boathouse of University College, together with that formerly used by Durham ARC but now the home of St Leonards and Durham Johnston Schools Clubs. Beyond in this drawing the river flows under Framwellgate Bridge, the second of the city's twelfth-century bridges, and on the right a glimpse of the castle's great hall leads the eyes, as they are led everywhere in Durham, to the mighty towers of the cathedral.

shallows restrict its value to odd scullers or tub pair. So crews usually turn before the old iron bridge, and Maiden Castle. At the crown of the next bend, where the old racecourse starts, is **Durham** ARC, 1860, its premises built around 1970 after the club moved from the original boathouse by Prebends Bridge. On the opposite bank rise Pelaw Woods, the gift of Lord Londonderry. The racecourse plain, venue for the annual Miners' Gala, marks now by a sapling the start of the regatta course, where once stood the Ash Tree.

There are, beside the official white line on the concrete wall, other faded lines which showed handicap intervals for the professional races at the regatta. At the end of Pelaw Woods stands the boathouse of **Collingwood** BC, formerly used by **St Hilds and Bede** BC, 1976, whose new boathouse is further downstream. On the other side of the river at the western end of the racecourse **St Cuthbert's Society** BC and the **Graduates Society** BC, 1974, share a red-brick boathouse. Just beyond, the Baths Bridge, replacing in 1962 an iron-girder one, provides a vantage position for both umpire and commentators' box during the regatta, for here is the short-course finish. The long course continues, taking in the New Elvet Bridge, constructed in 1975 to relieve traffic congestion in the city. Now begins the demanding bend.

On the north bank Brown's boathouse, dating from 1826, where the building and repair of racing boats has continued since the 1880s, stands opposite the Swan and Three Cygnets public house. Elvet Bridge itself comes next. Started by Bishop Pudsey in 1160, improved in 1225, repaired and widened in 1808, it is here that the challenge to crews is the greatest, for there is only six inches clearance on each side of the oars, while at the same time a turn has to be made virtually under the arch.

After Elvet Bridge Fearons Walk, made in the 1880s by a headmaster of Durham School to allow coaching by horseback, accompanies the river to the boathouse of **Hatfield** BC, 1885. Opposite, Dunelm House has at its base **Durham University** BC, 1877, WBC, 1980, and **Grey** BC, 1960. The modern structure is next to Ove Arup's Kingsgate footbridge, 1963, at the final bend called Bow Corner.

The last straight is beautifully wooded. The boathouse of **Van Mildert** BC, a college named after the Prince Bishop who founded the university, is followed by the Minute Tree signifying there is only another minute's rowing! **St Johns** and **St Chads** 1904 boathouses share a landing below St Oswald's Church. At the Count's House garden wall the long course comes to an end, though through graceful Prebends Bridge are further boathouses: **University College**, 1836, **Durham School**, 1847, amongst others. Then comes the weir, below, with its fulling-mill, and, soaring above, the majesty of the cathedral.

The regatta has featured much in this description, for it has been since 1834 the focus of Durham rowing. In the early days competitors nine abreast raced from Prebends Bridge to Pelaw Woods and back; fouling was allowed, though hands were forbidden to free the boats; spectators cheered their champions and threw missiles at the others!

In 1843 the first race between Town and Gown took place, and in 1854 the Grand Challenge Cup was inaugurated and soon became the most coveted prize in the North of England. Professional rowing did not end till 1946; even the dress regulations remained unaltered – 'clothing from the shoulders to below the knees, included a sleeved jersey'.

Another event in the regatta, the Wear Scurry, when coal-trimmers from the shipyards used shovels instead of blades, has disappeared, as have the NAR Handicaps. But eights, and of course women crews, have become an important part of this 'Henley of the North'.

There is other, no less popular, racing throughout the year, too. Durham City Regatta, formerly the Wear Regatta, has been held since 1970 under the aegis of Durham ARC, which also runs the Durham Small Boats Head of the River. The Wear Scullers Head began in 1976, and the Northern University Championships are further examples of the attraction this river has.

The verse of that old Durham University coach W.D. Lowe, 'Long as our river flows, Rowing tradition grows', cannot be more than an attempt to capture the magic of the Wear. Here indeed is a *dulce domum*.

IN 1954 there was a Veteran Regatta and Sports, which included Cumberland and Westmorland wrestling, to celebrate the 125th anniversary of **Talkin Tarn** ARC. This club representing rowing in Cumbria has held many regattas in its time, with special trains running from Carlisle, and 'streets' of tents set up to accommodate tradesmen as well as competitors. In fact, although the club was founded in 1859, regattas have been held on this beautiful water since 1849. There were not only races but also processions of illuminated boats, band concerts, wrestling, pole-leaping, hound trails and dog-walking.

The first boat was presented to the club by Lord Carlisle, its name *Lady Mary Howard* a reminder of the family association. The first boat bought by the club cost £15 in 1861; today there is another boat called *The Howard*, but its latest sculler cost, £1,800 in 1983.

The club has had many successful years: its junior members were in the National Championships during the 1970s, while in 1983 one junior sculler gained England representation. Women's rowing is now an integral part of the activities, with a trophy for the Ladies' Event at the principal regatta.

In 1967 the mile race, which necessitated the negotiation of a buoy at Tarn End, was discontinued, and the following year eights were introduced despite fears that the water might be too limiting.

For many years the club leased the Tarn from the Boothby Estates, employing a boatman and managing the lake with its surrounding woods. However, in 1975 on the sale of these areas to Cumbria County Council, the lease was relinquished, the pleasure boats were sold and the club became purely a user of the Tarn.

Inevitably there have been unhappy years during the club's life, but none more so than 1930 when two members of the Tarn's coxed four were drowned during a heat at Middlesbrough Regatta. Apparently the boat was swamped, neither could swim and, instead of keeping still, resting on their oars, they panicked. One of them had been a last-minute substitute, volunteering against the wishes of his relatives who perhaps were amongst the hundreds of spectators witnessing this tragedy. Happily, one of the three survivors was present at the 1984 regatta, still maintaining his association with the club.

OF THE MANY homes of rowing there are some which can claim a particular importance because of their place in the development of the sport. The River Tyne can undoubtedly be included in this group; indeed, a case could be made out for giving it pre-eminence as the cradle of rowing. Here great innovations were introduced, largely through the professional oarsmen of the last

14

century. In 1828 Brown and Emmett independently experimented with wooden outriggers, then two years later the latter, helped by Clasper, began using iron. Attention turned to the boat's keel, and once again a Tyne professional, Matthew Taylor, developed a

*The left-hand drawing of the River Tyne shows the stretch at Newburn where the regatta course ends. Beyond the bridge, looking downstream eastwards, the view includes the cooling-towers at Stella, marking the end of the straight. The twin chimneys each side of them belong to the Stella North and South power-stations, where the Northumberland Head of the River course finishes. Further downstream the great curve by Blaydon, forever associated with the races, leads to Scotswood Bridge, where the start for Tyne ARC Head of the River race may be found. Its finish upstream is the same as the regatta's, namely by the boathouses belonging to City of Newcastle RC and Tyne ARC itself. However, the start of the Northumberland Head is further upstream in Clara Vale, near that historic cottage, George Stephenson's birthplace.*

*A very different scene is presented in the right-hand drawing. This is of Talkin Tarn Country Park where Cumbria's only rowing club has been based for over 125 years. The setting is idyllic, and the tradition that the Tarn was bottomless or that it marked the site of another Brampton destroyed in an earthquake has not diminished the use of this beautiful water for sailing, windsurfing, diving, canoeing and of course rowing. It was bought by the county council in 1970, becoming a Country Park two years later.*

keel-less eight. His son introduced the cambered keel about 1870; Winship advocated the sliding seat, while the adoption of a mechanical runner, though not a Tyne invention, was enthusiastically taken up in 1871.

So the river engendered the evolution of today's racing shells, promoted new techniques and, above all, bred a racing fervour. Witness the huge following such an oar as Renforth attracted, and not only in his life on the water. When he died literally in a Canadian boat race, his body was brought back to Gateshead, and public subscription erected a monument as magnificent as that to Clasper in Whickham churchyard. Both men had funerals attended by thousands.

Today rowing uses the stretch between Scotswood Bridge and Clara Vale, but a century ago this part of the Tyne was useless for the great contests as it comprised myriad streams amid marsh. In those days it was the reach from the High Level Bridge in the centre of the city up to Scotswood where the champions battled. Now the various clubs have their boathouses upstream: the nearest to Scotswood just beyond the railway bridge is **Newcastle Royal Grammar School** BC, founded in 1938. After the curve by Blaydon comes the largely man-made Newburn Reach. Here at Stella, on the south bank **Newcastle University** BC, 1963, rows from base, while beyond the bridge the **City of Newcastle** RC and **Tyne** ARC, 1852, have their premises. This reach offers a straight 1,500-metre (just under a mile), four-lane course, possibly unsurpassed for regattas, the finish being upstream of the bridge. Beyond this point the river gently curves both ways till it arrives at Wylam. Here Stephenson's cottage, birthplace of the railway pioneer, marks the marshalling area for the start of the downstream Head of the River course, which runs 5,000 metres (3 miles) to Stella. The other Head course, organized by Tyne ARC, goes in the other direction from Scotswood to Newburn but it is the same distance.

These two heads are not the only events here. Mention has already been made of the admirable reach for regattas. There are two annually: the Tyne ARC 'At Home' and the much older Tyne Regatta, inaugurated in 1834, when the *Newcastle Journal* described the setting thus: 'The fine expanse of water extending from the

Kings Meadows to the elegant bridge at Scotswood was crowded with craft of every description – steam boats, pleasure boats, wherries, filled with gay company moving about in every direction. The fineness of the day and the novelty of the scene also drew an immense concourse of spectators to the banks of the river. On the Scotswood Road was a long line of carriages filled with the beauty and fashion of the town and district. The surprise is that with such facilities the Regatta should have been the first to be held upon the Tyne.' Well, it was not! The first competitive rowing dates back to 1821, on the occasion of George IV's coronation.

If this description reads like one of Henley, it is as well to remember that that regatta did not start for another five years, and to know that it was Tyne ARC that first took the name Leander.

CHAPTER TWO


*Yorkshire*

BRADFORD · WHITBY · YORK

THE REMARKABLE THING about the reach of the River Aire above
Hirst Weir, where the boathouse of **Bradford** ARC is situated,
must be that such a modest stretch should be home water to so
many West Yorkshire rowers. Picturesque it may be, but nobody
has ever disagreed that it is far from ideal, being a bare half mile, in
total, a regatta course that measures but just over a third of a mile
(600 metres), and less than a couple of cricket pitches at its widest
point.

Formed in 1867, the club started in the public boathouse at
Saltaire, restricting membership to twenty, probably because of
limited accommodation and equipment; indeed, the first mention of
competitive rowing in 1872 records that races were on a time basis,
each crew taking its turn in the only boat the club owned. In 1875 a
piece of land on the south bank opposite the present site was rented,
and a wood boathouse built for the five craft now available. Ten
years later another boathouse found its place beside the earlier one;
in 1893 yet a further, stone-built structure was erected on the
upstream side. Such extravagance brought its consequences; the
club suffered a decline up to World War I, and even after, for a
quarter of the membership was killed on active service. The land
rented changed hands, so the boathouse changed banks! Members
dismantled the structure, ferried it across to the new side and rebuilt
under the supervision of Geoffrey Saville-Smith. So it has
remained, a period-piece with its fireplaces, exposed roof timbers

18

*In this illustration of the River Aire at Hirst Weir, the buildings on the left are those used by Bradford Grammar School and Bradford ARC. On the other side of the river stands a mill, while out of the picture further to the right the Leeds and Liverpool Canal runs parallel to the river, its tree-lined bank affording a splendid setting for the finish of the regatta, and even, on occasion, the sight of a crew inadvertently shooting the weir itself.*

and, until 1968, lighting by hurricane and Tilley lamps.

After World War II prospects again looked black, the wood boatstore and all but one of the eights burned by vandals, the river choked with fallen trees. But new enthusiasm, new members, new achievements saved the club: Blues from Oxford and Cambridge joined, others after their rowing with **Bradford Grammar School BC**, 1954; even the Women's Squad at the Los Angeles Olympics was represented.

The regatta was growing; a second Autumn Sprint was introduced in 1978. Today all seems to be going well, even though the proximity of the weir means that occasionally crews finishing exhausted or elated find themselves unintentionally on a lower part of the river!

*Whitby, so picturesquely straddling the mouth of the River Esk, owes much of its attraction to the historic buildings on the east cliffs. Approached by some 199 steps the gallery-filled parish church has as its companions the ruins of a thirteenth-century abbey and a house whose enigmatic character seems so appropriate for a place that features in Bram Stoker's 'Dracula'. It is below these, surrounded by pantiled cottages, that the regatta is held. From seawards of the West Cliff the course makes its sharp turn to end away to the right of this illustration at the old Custom House. That final stretch will have taken the crews past the floating boathouse of Whitby Friendship ARC, bright in its red paint. Just behind it in the drawing the prominent balcony of the clubhouse may be identified, with the free-standing boathouse of Whitby Fishermen's ARC further along to the right.*

REASONS FOR the forming of rowing clubs range from the group of enthusiasts wishing to organize their energies to a less worthy desire to establish a select social élite. The foundation of **Whitby Friendship** ARC seems to have resulted from the dissatisfaction with the outcome of a single race.

From the time the Erimus Boating Club started in 1878, two factions developed, each declaring its superiority in rowing. So a race was arranged, using the old heavy four-oared gigs, on a four mile course from Sandsend to Whitby Bridge. The crew of *Wild Drake* lost to that of *Water Lily* by 1½ minutes, but as a result the former's supporters, mainly working-class youths, broke away from Erimus and somewhat oddly named their new club 'Friendship'. The strange thing is that they really made the club a success, and Erimus faded away. The lads paid for their first gig within a year, forbade drink and swearing and even included in their rules: 'All business be kept a perfect secret'.

By hiring a warehouse in Green Lane and wheeling the boat down the Cinder Ghaut to the water, rowing was possible, and in 1883, four years old, the club won its first regatta race. It also received a cheque for £5 from the Maharajah Duleep Singh!

The regatta was in fact a revival of Whitby's own, which had first been held back in the 1840s, and it is good to note that within a year or two Erimus and Friendship were working together organizing additional racing.

By 1894 the club was desperate for boathouse accommodation at the water, and the solution came in the form of a lighter moored below Tin Ghaut, though the following year a dispute arose with the harbour trustees because the craft bore advertising. Such problems are not new, it seems.

In 1912 another club, the Whitby Amateur, was formed, catering particularly for the fishermen's love of the four-oar gig. But by 1929 it too had gone.

A new boathouse was purchased in 1910, or rather built by members from materials purchased. In 1937 another club, the Whitby Fisherman's ARC, was welcomed as a new competitor, to join the traditional rivals of Scarborough.

Like the Friendship, the regatta has had its lean years, but today it seems as popular as it ever was. The course of 1¼ miles begins opposite Upgang Chine, past Blade Steps, with a finishing line opposite the Old Custom House on the River Esk; the senior start is further along the coast at Newholm Beck, but all have the turning buoy at the entrance or extension of the harbour.

Even if the heavy gigs have gone, there are still the fixed-seat craft with a four-foot beam. Perhaps one should be called *Endeavour* or *Resolution* after the ships built for Captain Cook, who learned his seamanship in Whitby; or perhaps one could be named *Dracula*, for was it not here that part of Bram Stoker's book was set?

THE FIRST recorded rowing event at York took place in 1843 on a course downstream of the present regatta; a second was organized in 1844, both for professionals. A third, in 1863, arranged by the 16th Queen's Lancers then stationed at the Cavalry Barracks, used

*Much of York's rowing is based between Lendal Bridge, 1863, and the more modern Clifton Bridge, upstream. The top left drawing shows the former, with its water tower; while the lower scene is also taken from Lendal Bridge looking across to the Museum Gardens that provide so attractive a background of trees for the finishes of the regattas and the Yorkshire Head. It is by this Bridge York City boathouse stands, and on the opposite bank a little way upstream the boathouse of Ripon and York St John College is to be found. Further upstream, beyond the Scarborough Bridge that carries the railway, St Peter's School has its boathouse.*

*The right hand drawing illustrates the position of Lendal Bridge, at the top and its nearness to the Minster. Rowing at York is fortunate to have so central an access.*

the Fulford stretch of the Ouse adjacent to their quarters.

Then in 1865 the York Amateur RC, having been formed two years earlier, held its first regatta, again at Fulford. That was the predecessor of today's regatta, though the course moved upstream to its present venue in 1905. Shortly after the club's inception, a breakaway group formed the White Rose ARC, with its own boathouse adjacent to a swimming-pool, the city's first, at the end of Marygate. However, at the turn of the century the White Rose Club fell on hard times and decided to rejoin York Amateurs, and the name was then changed to **York City** RC. The White Rose boathouse was later occupied by **St John's College** BC and has since been rebuilt.

The annual regattas continued from 1905, with the White Rose trophy joining the Londesborough Challenge Cup. Records of club activity are sparse because in 1947 the Ouse flooded to a height of seventeen feet nine inches above summer level and, according to the subsequent minute entry, members had to secure the boathouse to nearby lamposts and telegraph poles as it was floating off its foundations; then in 1954 the replacement club premises were destroyed by fire; so what water failed to do fire completed, and the only records from 1946 are minute books.

A decision was then taken to move the site of the boathouse nearer to the city, on the opposite side of the river, so that the public and social activity could develop. Provision was also made for ladies' rowing. From 1954 till the new accommodation became available two years later, St Peter's School BC played host, thus cementing the close ties between the two clubs. Perhaps the school was aware of one past pupil, Guy Fawkes! Anyway, as only one boat was saved from the fire, 1956 saw the club now in a new building, together with the task of creating a new fleet of boats.

The original site was eventually taken over by **Archbishop Holgate's Grammar School** BC, itself hosted by York City in 1957. Such hospitality was also extended to the embryo **York University** BC when it began in 1965.

Today York City is well established. Its situation on the Ouse permits use of some twenty miles of unrestricted river, even if present-day pleasure boating can be a problem. Some comfort may be taken from the 1865 *Yorkshire Gazette* reporting that steampackets and pleasure boats 'got into the Regatta Course destroying the interest and causing spectators to express anger at such foolish conduct'.

The Ouse now supports three regattas organized by York City: a Small Boats Head is held $2\frac{1}{2}$ miles upstream from Fulford Village Green, and a $3\frac{3}{4}$ mile course downstream from Rawcliffe to the city centre has the Yorkshire Head.

Past members of the club here included at least one Olympic silver medallist, but what is equally important is that the people who organize also have had distinction in that, of the five members who have been Regatta Secretary since 1946, two became Lord Mayor of the city and a third was chairman of York District Sports Council.

**St Peter's School** BC was founded about 1840. One of its earliest members, John Richardson became President of CUBC and rowed no. 7 in the winning boat in 1845 when for the first time the University Boat Race took place on the Putney to Mortlake course.

Rowing at St Peter's continued through the 1850s but there is no record of races until 1864, when the school beat a crew of university men. In this century successes have followed: in the 1960s and 70s the Yorkshire Head was won in five successive years, and the school competed regularly in regattas as distant as London.

Since it started, the club has rowed on the Ouse; its present boathouse, built in the 1960s, is but the latest in a series on Clifford Long Reach, and all have had to contend with flooding. Upstream the river meanders gently through the 'Ings', or banked meadows; downstream under the Clifton, Scarborough and Lendal Bridges. Here then may be seen the boys and girls of the club on the water, today in fours or pairs only, as eights are less common in Yorkshire and the North generally. There is still a healthy rivalry with Durham, Bradford Grammar and Lancaster Royal Grammar Schools, while its success in city regattas is perhaps some consolation for its current absence from Henley.

# CHAPTER THREE

## North-West

### CHESTER · HOLLINGWORTH LAKE · LANCASTER LIVERPOOL · SALFORD

'OUR BEAUTIFUL RIVER, smooth as a lake, and at all times full, seems to invite this manly pastime; and I can safely appeal to all who have eyes to see and hearts to feel whether the light skiffs gliding over the surface do not add to the charm of a landscape which in this country has few rivals.' So ended a letter in the *Chester Gazette* in response to the news that a month or two earlier, in May 1838, the gentlemen oars of the city had decided to organize their hitherto extemporary activity into a club, to be called the Chester Victoria RC in honour of the young Queen. It was formally established at a meeting in the Castle, and a few days later some seventy members enrolled.

However, by 1843 dedicated training seems to have lost its appeal, and five years later the club was almost at an end. Revival came in 1851, with vigorous fund-raising to obtain a new boathouse, and the turning point was reached when in 1854 Mat Taylor, the ship's carpenter from the Tyne, became trainer to what was by now the **Royal Chester** RC. His contribution was of national rather than local importance, for he made the famous *Victoria* keel-less boat which enabled the club in the following year to take the Wyfold and Stewards' Cups at Henley.

Today Royal Chester's boathouse at the Groves continues to offer the successors of those 'young men of the city' of 1838 the opportunity to enjoy this river. But back in the last century such young men who could not call themselves gentlemen were denied

*The Groves at Chester provide the base for rowing in this city, whose Roman founders must surely have taken to the river too. This view looks upstream from the boathouses of the King's School, and Royal Chester, to the sweeping bend of the Dee. High up on the bank St Peter's Church dominates the neighbouring houses, some of which have become familiar by their colour as significant landmarks to crews on the water. The opposite bank gives onto a vast flood plain, echoing the Roodee lower downstream where the racecourse is and affording no shelter from the prevailing south-west wind. It must be added that the 1923 Queen's Park suspension bridge, though graceful, similarly treats spectators watching the finish here.*

memberships of the Royals, so consequently another club was founded, in 1869, taking as the name **Grosvenor** RC.

There is a third boathouse at the Groves, that of the **King's School** RC. First mention of the club was in 1883, but it does not appear to have had a boathouse until 1925, and then it was rented, at Dee Hills Park. By 1946 the school boats were sharing Grosvenor's. In 1954 the premises of the Cestria BC at the White House Hotel in Sandy Lane became available, though the eights used Royals, and as if to mark this independence a sectional clinker eight was bought, possibly the first in the country. Then in 1960 came the final move to the Chester Boat Company's site. The following decade was rich in success: National Schools Regatta, National Championships, international events.

Nor should it be forgotten that there are other clubs: **Queens**

*The left-hand illustration shows the third home of rowing at Chester, the Grosvenor. Founded in 1869 to redress the social imbalance, this club provided rowing facilities for the working class. It is strange therefore to observe the opulence of its clubhouse, reminiscent of the Tyrol, and note that the accompanying boathouse, opened in 1982 by the Duke of Westminster, prominently displays the Grosvenor arms. The Boat House Inn, beyond, allows a glimpse of the more prosaic boathouses of King's and Royal.*

*Inside the Royal Chester's social club, pictured in the right-hand drawing, there are some good examples of the type of shields seen in older clubs. Here the successes record the 1892 Stewards and the 1924 Wyfold Challenge Cups at Henley, and they echo those magnificent winners' boards at Chester racecourse.*

**Park High School**, formerly Chester City Grammar School, **Athena**, originally for girls of the Queen's School, and **Rex**, the Old Boys from King's.

Gentleman and artisans, women and boys, they all met at the Chester Regatta. It is uncertain when the first regatta was held – one reference suggests 1773, and another 1814, but the clearest description is dated 1817, where 'Liverpool and other aquatic-minded cities sent boats' crews to compete in the races.' There is a poster of 1832 advertising events for six- and four-oar gigs, and one for women in fishermen's boats. In the 1840 regatta there was even a coracle race, as well as the usual gigs and skiffs. One interesting facet was the presence of policemen who 'will be afloat in order to keep the course clear, and others will also be stationed in the meadows to prevent persons trespassing in the hay grass'.

Nor is the regatta the only event. There are long-distance sculls, a veterans' regatta, a women's regatta and of course the North of England Head of the River. This last was begun in 1935 and had twelve crews in it. Two years later Clare College established a record time of fourteen minutes fifty-nine seconds from the start at Eccleston Ferry to the Groves, a distance of $3\frac{1}{4}$ miles, and in 1982 Agecroft managed 15.03 minutes. The Dee may not be 'covered with boats decorated in all the gaudy splendour' of earlier years, but it is as busy as ever.

WHEN THE RAILWAYS opened up the coastal resorts in the 1830s and 40s, they also gave inland places opportunity to attract holidaymakers. One such was Hollingworth Lake, 'the weavers' seaport'. Its purpose was primarily as a reservoir for the Rochdale Canal, but almost from the year of its construction, 1794, pleasure boating appeared on its water, thanks largely to the Rochdale visitors. Then, some fifty years later, the Canal Company found in a lakeside entrepreneur, Henry Newall, just the person to develop the recreational potential of this spot. By 1856 two paddle-steamers, two hotels and a boathouse were all contributing to the popularity of the lake. A regatta was organized after a few years, running the customary aquatic sports, and in 1872 **Hollingworth Lake** RC came into existence, with of course Mr Newall as its president. A

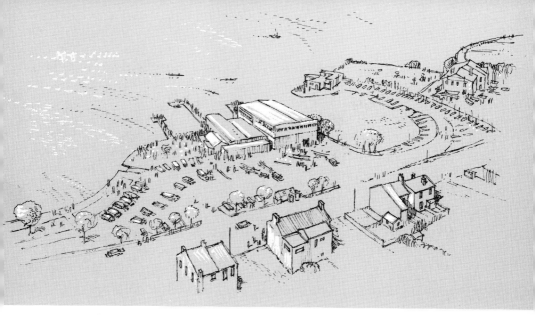

*In 1895 Hollingworth Lake rowing moved across the water from the site it had occupied since its formation in 1872 — or, to be more accurate, its reformation, for there had been a club here in 1862. By 1973 the building was demolished and another, half as large again, arose. The regatta has been an annual event since 1964, with its course a straight 800 metres. But once again to be accurate, there have been at least two years when it was not held: 1973 and 1984. In 1985 the lake was drained to allow the dams to be repaired, so the rowing had to be wherever the club could place boats.*

new boathouse was erected, responsibility for the annual regatta was assumed and a bright prospect for racing on the lake seemed assured.

By the time its Diamond Jubilee arrived in 1932, those hopes had been realized. Additions were made to the boathouse, and no fewer than sixteen trophies found their way there before World War II stopped the procession. When peace returned, Hollingworth took up where it left off: not only did the successes continue but, even more important, new members were attracted to so thriving a club.

Centenary year saw further improvements to the premises, where new international-standard oarsmen could be found amongst its users.

*Lancaster marks its association with John of Gaunt by the rowing club's name. In this drawing the boathouse on the Lune, from which the city derives its own name, can be seen on the right. The broad sweep of the river leads eventually to the Quay, below Castle Hill on which stand not only the Norman fortress and gaol but also the Priory Church of St Mary. There is something reminiscent of Durham in the composition. Upstream the waters used for rowing are crossed by the magnificent aqueduct built in 1797 to carry Rennie's Preston to Kendal canal, and by the much more recent M6 motorway bridge.*

THE ORIGINAL TOWN CLUB in Lancaster was formed in 1842, rowing from the quayside on the tidal stretch of the River Lune. At first its base was the former Royal Blue Anchor Hotel, but after three years permission was granted, by 'the Lords of Skerton' to build a boathouse on the 'wasteland above Skerton Mill'. So began the association with a site that has lasted to this day.

Political animosity infected the club to such an extent in 1866 that the members dissolved it, reforming into two clubs: a new Lancaster RC which moved across the river to premises now occupied by **Lancaster Royal Grammar School** BC, formed 1948, and the **John O'Gaunt** RC, which stayed on at Skerton. In 1883 the old wooden boathouse was replaced by one built of stone, and it signalled a renaissance in the club's fortune. Membership increased to 250; in 1901 a second storey and dock extension came; hospitality being given to the school and university clubs at their inception. But by 1976 a new boathouse was once again needed and so in 1983, exactly a hundred years after its predecessor, the present building was opened.

There are reports of regattas at Lancaster in 1801, though the City Regatta did not begin till 1842, on the tidal stretch of the river starting from the quay below Castle Hill. Like so many, it had a puny programme but was a great social and civic occasion. And also like others, its popularity declined after a few years, was revived and, after the Diamond Jubilee of Queen Victoria celebration regatta, maintained its new momentum.

Lancaster, elevated to a city in 1936, might be a somewhat minor place compared with the great centres of population but in the history of rowing it has a secure niche. In 1870 one of its crews, the *Duffer*, came to Henley Royal Regatta determined to try out a new principle. This was to have larger than normal fixed seats, lightly greased pants and a technique which involved sliding up and down on the seat. The crew managed to reach the final of the Stewards' Challenge Cup, 'going like a piston and a pair of scissors' as one commentator put it, and, though it was narrowly defeated by Oxford Etonians, the principle of sliding 'seats' – of whatever kind – was established.

IN THE 1880s a few friends wanting to secure preferential renting rates from boat-hirers on the then rural West Float inlet on the Wirral side of the Mersey formed themselves into a club, taking the Victoria Tower nearby for its name. Thus in 1884 **Liverpool Victoria** RC broke away from hiring and established itself further up the inlet, only to find that increasing dock development posed a threat. While other rowing clubs succumbed, 'Vics' prudently acquired land from the dock corporation well away from any possible development, so that today, even though there has been an encroachment, the club still retains its facility and plenty of good rowing water. There are plans to establish a water-sports centre somewhere in the dock area, and doubtless 'Vics' will play a leading role in its birth. Meanwhile it continues to provide a rowing presence on the Mersey, while in the wider scene it has provided the ARA with its first provincial, 'grass-roots' president.

Further evidence of the club's concern for promoting rowing

here can be traced in the hospitality it offered to what was then Wallasey Grammar School BC in 1922. Today, as the **Henry Meoles School** BC, it has its own boathouse standing beside the 'Vics', the result of **Liverpool University** BC's moving to Knowsley in 1980.

Another home of rowing is **Sefton RC**, formed in 1958 primarily for ex-pupils of **Merchant Taylors** BC at Litherland, Liverpool, both clubs rowing on the very restricted water of the Leeds-Liverpool canal.

If there is one person who has contributed most to all these clubs on the Mersey, it must be F.J. ('Pop') Grant, the almost legendary captain of the 'Vics' earlier this century.

*One of the few rowing clubs to be based in a dock area, Liverpool Victoria has its boathouse at West Float, Birkenhead. Despite the proximity of ships, cranes and all the accompanying maritime appurtenances, this oasis of sport manages to preserve its identity and find in such an environment opportunities to row, even if it means at night.*

*This illustration of Agecroft Regatta shows the boathouse built in 1935 and its first floor that was added fifty years later. Such a terse description does not do justice to the tenacity this club has shown through these years, for it is the only survivor of fifteen that once used the River Irwell at Salford. Its further claim to a place in the sport's history is that it was the last to hold fixed-seat rowing.*

MANY ROWING CLUBS look back to an inaugural meeting at a town hall, a titled person in the chair, and an election of numerous officials, and committees, not to mention the formulation of elaborate rules. How refreshing then to learn of the birth of **Agecroft** RC: just a few friends getting together to row and enjoy it. That was in 1861, when Ishmael Lythgoe decided that the River Irwell at Agecroft was just the place to keep a boat.

Soon a boathouse was built, colours were adopted, a course was selected for racing. In 1865 the first recorded race took place, probably from Agecroft Bridge to Douglas Green Weir and back, making a 2½-mile stretch. The following year saw the start of Agecroft Regatta, when a four-oar race also involved turning, and as three boats entered there must have been some problems at the buoy. A bigger problem came at the end of that year, for the boathouse was swept away by exceptional floods. Undeterred, the club built another at Douglas Green, in the short space of a fortnight and at a cost of £147, including landing stage. This was no temporary shed, for it was used until 1935.

By 1874 the regatta attracted sixteen clubs; there were thirty-two races, and prizes totalled £135. However, the river progressively deteriorated: in the thirty-second regatta, 1904, there were only twenty entries for rowing on this 'creeping, crawling slippery slimy horror', as the newspaper put it. Things could only improve after that.

Agecroft survived, the sole remaining club out of some fifteen. It even adopted sliding seats eventually, though it was the last club to give up fixed-seat rowing.

Today the Manchester Ship Canal, over a century old itself, is in the stage of redundancy, with the Company winding up its operations. Agecroft sees the opportunity of using the docks and continuation of the River Irwell into the city centre as new club waters, or more correctly as old waters. For this stretch goes to the place where Nemesis RC had its boathouse, and the public house that has been built there is called the Mark Addy, after the local hero who saved fifty-one lives from the river; he himself was an Agecroft RC member. One life he reputedly saved was Lythgoe's!

CHAPTER FOUR


*East Midlands*

BURTON · DERBY · NOTTINGHAM

ALONG STAPENHILL ROAD, Burton-on-Trent, three rowing clubs
have their base. The oldest, **Burton Leander** RC, was founded in
1847 thus giving it a seniority exceeded by fewer than half-a-dozen
others in the country. However, its boathouse is younger, being
once owned by another club, the Burton RC, formed in 1865 and
dissolved in 1920. Leander purchased it, having moved from its
original clubhouse at the Old Mill, Newton Road and then the
Forge, to premises opposite Scalpcliff Road. In 1980 the building
was further extended, giving more space for boats at ground level,
while on the first floor a lecture room, training and other facilities
have been added. But Leander does not keep this all to itself, for it
offers accommodation to another, much younger club, formed in
1976: **Bass** RC does not need explanation in this town.
　Nearer to the bridge, **Trent** RC boathouse presents a contrast in
style that reflects the club's origin in 1863, for here there was a
common divide, the membership being largely that of the artisan
and manual worker, in contrast to Leander's salaried, gentleman
class. Having evolved from the activities of the eighteenth century
Trent navigators, Trent RC has always been egalitarian, a
characteristic which almost brought its downfall in 1889 when it
found itself on the wrong side of the 'mechanics' rule divide. But
having refused to eject its labourer members, its president Percy
Evershed, a local brewing industrialist, was at the forefront in
creating the National Amateur Rowing Association. The new

*This view from Burton's town bridge shows Trent and Burton Leanders boathouses on the left; in the distance is Drakelow power-station; and on the right the towers of the parish church and Bass brewery.*

boathouse was built in 1908, and the inter-war years saw many rowers using its facilities. Successes in the next quarter of a century were not prolific though the club did produce a dual Henley winner and European bronze medallist. In 1981 expansion of membership resulted in an extension of the boathouse, as well as representation in the 1984 Anglo-French junior competition. This development programme continues with the proposal to construct a further boathouse and gymnasium on the site of the original building adjacent to the Trent bridge.

Important as these boathouses are, and Leander is justly proud of its, the focus of Burton's rowing must undoubtedly be the regatta. One of the few remaining traditional tented regattas in the provinces, it has been run, since 1866, by a committee rather than particular clubs. In that first year the President, elected by the committee made up of the existing New Leander, as it was then called, Burton and Trent Clubs, was the Marquess of Anglesey; interestingly, this association continued till 1972, when the Seventh

*Two very different bridges feature in these drawings. The left-hand one is of Ferry Bridge at Burton-on-Trent, which marks the regattas finish. Built in 1889 to replace a ferryboat that plied between Stapenhill and Burton, its contribution to the character of the regatta is considerable. And that is all the more appropriate because this event continues to be a tented occasion, not centred on any boathouse. Not without reason, too, it has become clearly associated with refreshment, being represented on the labels for Trent Bitter.*

*The other bridge, in the right-hand drawing, once carried a railway line across the Derwent, but today it has an even more important function in providing an excellent position for the umpire at Derby City regatta. From here a clear view downstream to the start is possible, not only for that official but for spectators too. Upstream there is this equally rewarding view of the two boathouses belonging to Derby and Derwent clubs.*

Marquess resigned the office. With the patrons including such names as Allsopp, Bass Ratcliff and Worthington, there was little doubt the occasion was a festive opportunity for the whole town.

Nevertheless, the regatta had its problems: for one thing, it was held away from the boatclubs' premises; for another, the river stretch it did use became over the years more polluted, so much so in fact that there was a time in the 1950s when foam from industrial effluent would spill over the gunwales, and the prospect of pitching into the water with its untreated sewage daunted many a crew. So in 1965 the medieval weir went, the river was opened up and cleansed, allowing rowing to be done over a longer continual distance from the Trent Bridge to Walton; going any further had proved disastrous in 1958 when one of Leander's eights was crushed on the Walton Bridge.

A seemingly imminent disaster, in 1971, was turned to advantage when torrential rain meant abandoning the regatta. But rather than miss a year it was held on the Sunday following Henley's, and became an instant success. Three years later a riverside fête joined the occasion. There's no knowing what next to expect in the Burton Regatta: already it has attracted crews from Canada, Hong Kong, the USA and Zambia. Perhaps one year it will see Leander racing Burton Leander.

DARLEY PARK on the north side of Derby has the River Derwent flowing through its sweeping grassland. Mature trees and a gentle slope to the river give it a feeling of history as well as seclusion from the throbbing city. When, around 1783, the weirs at Darley and below St Mary's Bridge were constructed, a stretch of water was there for the asking, so it is not surprising that some kind of regatta took place in the 1840s. The year 1859, then, saw the regatta revived with a scullers' race for amateurs living within twenty miles and a Stewards' Cup for fours within sixty miles; the following year the geographical limits must have been relaxed, for crews came from Richmond-on-Thames and Newcastle, the latter using a forty-two-foot clasper. Professional watermen raced too, until 1863.

By 1875 the regatta was showing signs of a relapse, perhaps partly due to the construction here of the railway bridge by the Great

*Derby city regatta is centred in Darley Park, a beautifully wooded area with grassy slopes leading down to the river. In this view looking downstream, both permanent and temporary features contribute to its delightful character: the former railway bridge, the sixteenth-century tower of the cathedral, St Mary's RC Church, the boathouses of Derby and Derwent clubs, and the marquees and sideshows of the regatta itself, all these amongst mature trees, with a glimpse upstream of Darley Abbey.*

Northern Company. In 1877 its attraction was giving enough concern that **Derwent** RC, which had, soon after its formation in 1857, done so much to organize the event, must have wondered if its new boathouse, started in 1862, would ever be completed as the base for the regatta.

However, in 1879 an ally had been born, **Derby** RC. At first its boathouse was a wooden shed built with timbers from a circus, but, finally overcoming the objections from the Great Northern Railway, another wooden structure arose, in 1893, capped by a corrugated iron roof supplied by Handysides who had built the iron bridge itself.

In 1894 joint races were held in the summer with Derwent; both clubs contributed to the Lifeboat Day parade and gala in Darley Park. Understandably therefore in 1903 there was a proposal at a meeting between the Derwent and Derby members to revive the town regatta. Both regatta and clubs flourished, so far as rowing was concerned. The problems seemed to centre more on the boathouses. Derwent's was almost entirely destroyed by fire in 1935, the boats and equipment being saved by the efforts of some members of Derby RC who happened to be at the river; Derby itself, after an agonizingly long-drawn-out wait for its new site, in 1962, when the move across the river promised to be difficult, found that providentially the water froze, giving enough thickness to the ice to permit boats, timber, seats and all the equipment to be carried over. Small wonder that such good fortune spurred the club to enter for Henley the next year, and reach a final. However, not all was benign, for later that year a clinker boat's bows ran into another crew, puncturing the first man's thorax. As a result the committee ordered that all boats be fitted with rubber ball, a measure later taken up by the ARA.

In 1965 Derby won at Henley, the Wyfold Cup setting the seal on its eighty-five years of rowing at Darley Park.

*Trent Bridge, Nottingham, has a significance for more than one sport, and this view of the downstream side shows the home of two. The floodlight standards are for the ground used by Nottingham Forest Football Club, while to the right rowing has its representation in the three boathouses of Nottingham Britannia, Nottingham, and Nottingham & Union.*

*In some ways the focus of Nottingham's rowing has moved 3½ miles to Holme Pierrepont, where since 1972 the sport has found a new home. It is here at the National Water Sports Centre that major international championships, as well as many club regattas are now held. Though the course may be, as this drawing suggests, a somewhat featureless stretch of water, time will doubtless remedy the landscape's starkness, and this view up the 2,000 metres to the start could become as characterful as many of the more historic sites.*

TRENT BRIDGE, NOTTINGHAM, has a significance for more than one sport, and as a home of rowing its history goes back well into last century. The oldest club owes its origin to the activities of a few young men who, going out together in a hired rowing boat, decided to call themselves the Nautilus Rowing Club. Becoming more established, they rented a site on the Trent side and in 1862 changed their name to Nottingham Rowing Club. On the opposite bank the Union RC was flourishing socially if not aquatically, though it did enter for the Wyfold at Henley and indeed in 1928 had an Olympic success at Amsterdam. However, by the end of World War II, despite a good fleet of boats and a sound financial position, amalgamation was in the air. Thus the **Nottingham and Union** RC came into being. A founder member, Sir John Turney, presented a magnificent cup, and success, at home and nationally, was assured.

In 1869 another club began catering for canoeing as well as rowing, with premises at the Trent Navigation Wharf, moved in 1911 to the present site next to Forest football ground. By this time canoeing had faded away, though the same, **Nottingham Britannia** RC, reputedly owes its origin to the canoeists meeting at the Britannia Inn. At Henley the Royal Regatta includes in its programme the Britannia Cup for coxed fours, a reminder of the club's centenary celebrations. Interestingly, the club's first president was a Mr W. Earp, though not, it must be admitted, the legendary Wyatt!

The third club on Trentside, **Nottingham** BC, resulted from a breakaway group of Nottingham RC who took a boat out on a Sunday and, refusing to apologize for thus contravening the club rules, set up their own club in 1894. Indeed, that first outing on a Sunday was commemorated further by an oil painting of the rebels, who included a future Lord Mayor of the city. However, in 1912 the boathouse was gutted by fire, the work it must be said of suffragettes, not the parent club! In retaliation members went to the women's next meeting and, according to reports, 'subjected them to embarrassment and indignity'.

By the 1930s some fourteen senior sculling trophies had been won, and the club sponsored High Pavement School junior rowing, while from 1946 to 1951 Nottingham University's boats were housed here until their premises were built. During the last quarter of a century many successes have been recorded: over a hundred national championships and twenty international medals, as well as a Diamond Sculls and Wyfold.

The city's regatta dates from before 1850; the head and scullers head races are more recent. They of course use the Trent, but not far away at Holme Pierrepont the National Water Sports Centre provides the venue for the Nottingham International Regatta. In 1970 excavation of the gravelpits began, eventually, and at a total

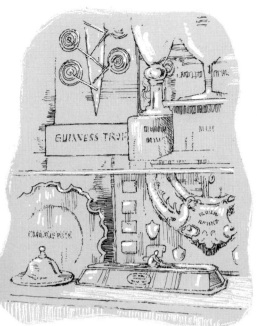

*There is no denying that the National Water Sports Centre has every facility, and these drawings illustrate but two: on the right the impressive judging tower, opposite the finish of the Olympic-standard 2,000 metre course is linked to the centre building with its short-stay accommodation, changing-rooms, shop, restaurant and bars; the left-hand drawing shows that Holme Pierrepont also displays another aspect of rowing. Amongst the rewards can be seen such examples as the Guinness Trophy, the Penny Chuter Salver, the Darby Trophy for Senior Sculls and the Four Oar Challenge Trophy.*

cost of £400,000, resulting in a mile and a quarter (2,000-metre watercourse of six lanes comparable with Olympic standards, the depth of nine feet ($2\frac{1}{2}$ metres) and width of forty-four feet ($13\frac{1}{2}$ metres), together with sloping sides, ensure a minimum of wave interference, and fairness in lanes.

So fine a stretch of still water attracts not only rowing but also sailing, fishing, powerboat racing, water-skiing, sailboard and canoeing activities. All this is set in a country park of 270 acres with a nature reserve, camping sites and conference centre, making it less a 'home' and more a 'mansion' of rowing!

43

CHAPTER FIVE

## West Midlands and Wales

SHREWSBURY · IRONBRIDGE · BEWDLEY
STOURPORT · WORCESTER · BIRMINGHAM
STRATFORD-UPON-AVON · EVESHAM · HEREFORD
ROSS-ON-WYE · PENARTH

THERE HAS BEEN rowing on the Severn at Shrewsbury for over 150 years, and it cannot be denied that the river has played an important role in the town's growth. Nowhere is this better seen than at the generous bend which has the Quarry on the east and Shrewsbury School high up on the west side. At the foot of this bank stands the boathouse of the **Royal Shrewsbury School** BC. Admittedly the many bends in the river have proved something of a disadvantage in both racing and training, though the excellent towpath compensates slightly for the latter. The 500 metres straight (about a third of a mile) has seen many a tight contest and will be familiar to countless crews both from the school and further distant.

An early reference to rowing at the school is in letters written by boys: 1828 saw a race between 'Gentlemen of the Six Oar' and 'Snobs of Jobson's Boat', in spite of the headmaster, Dr Butler, forbidding boating and threatening prosecution to persons hiring them to boys. However, by 1830 the junior boys seem to have had an established tradition of taking boats upriver before breakfast, and by 1839 the first school regatta took place, continuing till 1891 and attracting a varied entry. There were eights, sixes, fours and threes – that is, a 'randan' of sculls and two oars; there were bumping races and a Procession of Boats, the craft being locked together,

44

*The Toll Bridge at Shrewsbury was the viewing place for this drawing, looking upstream to where the Severn's great encircling bend passes the Quarry on the town side, and on the other Shrewsbury School. The latter looks down to its boathouse, which has as a neighbour that of Pengwern a short distance along the bank. Incidentally, the school, founded in 1552, moved here only a hundred years ago to what had been originally a foundling hospital and subsequently a workhouse. So, in a sense, rowing has been here longer than the school.*

oars upright and crews singing 'Heart of Oak' and 'God Save the Queen'.

In 1866 the school boat club set about providing for itself a boathouse instead of having to use Harwood's, which was some 300 yards upstream, and it must be proud to recall that many years later, in 1927, the Oxford University eight travelled here to be coached by A.E. Kitchin. Perhaps this is the only time the University has departed from Isis and Thames.

More recent years have seen the school's rowing successes grow, particularly at Henley in the Princess Elizabeth Cup and the Special race for schools. The regatta continues as an event for the town, still bringing to the Quarry colour and excitement. But perhaps the

The massive cooling-towers of Buildwas power-station are a reminder that Ironbridge's industrial history is continuous. They overlook the 1863 Albert Edward Railway Bridge and the boathouse of Ironbridge RC, which moved upriver in 1912 from a location near the famous Ironbridge itself. The regatta start is now opposite the power-station, its finish at Regatta Meadow, and its course still enjoys the same wooded banks that Abram Darby knew in those years which saw the birth of Britain's Industrial Revolution here.

Bewdley, also on the Severn, is the subject of the second drawing. Now the character is very different, with stately eighteenth-century houses lining Severnside South, and as this view from the rowing club boathouse shows, on Severnside North the picturesque half-timbered cottages of a pre-industrial age. It is at Dog Lane, which runs at the end of this range once known as Cole's Quay, that the regatta course finishes.

46

health of Shrewsbury rowing owes not a little to the thirty years' service of its boatsman, Gerry Sturges, who has repaired the older wooden boats and built many pairs and scullers.

This account of rowing at Shrewsbury should not omit mention of another club, **Pengwern** BC. That 1839 regatta included an eight whose crew was a mixture of boys and 'Townsmen who thought they could row': such a disparaging description of possibly the Pengwern oarsmen was atoned for later by the presence of an umpire boat at the regatta whose occupants wore the uniform of the 'Shrewsbury Boating Club', the probable predecessor of Pengwern. Anyway, the club, formally founded in 1871, can be proud of its equality with Royal Shrewsbury in the fine location of its boathouse.

THAT STRETCH of the Severn between Shrewsbury and Bridgnorth includes the historic Coalbrookdale, justly termed the cradle of industrial Britain. It has also been, for over a century, the nursery of many oarsmen. For example, in 1868 the annual schools race between Shrewsbury and Cheltenham was held at Bridgnorth, generating such interest in rowing that **Bridgnorth** RC was born, and within three months its crew entered for the Ironbridge Regatta. Two years later a challenge race starting at Buildwas Ford was arranged between Bridgnorth and Ironbridge. The home crew's 'well-trained stroke ensured an early victory', but more important the event demonstrates the existence of **Ironbridge** RC. Indeed, only ten years were to elapse before the long service of a Bridgnorth member started as Captain of Ironbridge, and the carnival fêtes which had enlivened the waters from Buildwas to Albert Bridge gave place in 1883 to the Ironbridge Regatta. Whether this occasion represented an improvement in decorum might be questioned, as one of the events, the Goose Race, saw the competitors dressed in 'university running costume', the geese liberated midriver, and the chase over land and water.

In those days the boathouse was on a field rented from Lord Forester, but soon a new corrugated iron shed was erected. The club and regatta advanced in status and popularity, particularly as the attendant sports included such entertainment as tightrope-walkers and fire-eaters from Sanger's Circus. By 1891 over 4,000

47

people paid for admission. Yet such is the unpredictability of financial health that at the end of the next year the club's bank account was but 37 shillings. However, that was after new boats had been paid for.

Once again fortunes changed: apathy reigned and the regatta disappeared from the calendar. Competitive racing gave place to pleasure boating, resulting not only in the lack of incentive to go to other regattas but also in the resiting of the boathouse. Now it was to be by the Albert Edward Railway Bridge upstream, the structure formally opened in 1914. A club regatta had been held the previous autumn, but the war soon put a stop to such things, although water excursions were organized for convalescent soldiers.

However, times improved, and by 1926 an open regatta was back. But once again, after a gradual improvement in both membership and successes, war intervened. The club's boats were commandeered by the Army for barbed-wire laying, and when in 1940 remaining members tried to row they were told the water down to the old bridge was a restricted area. However, by logging each row, the police were placated!

In 1950 another start was made with an open regatta, and crews were attracted from enough clubs to give an average entry of fifty-five over the period till 1963, even when the Kynnersley Cup for sculls was mislaid at the time of the Meadow Inn change of ownership, and never recovered!

This was not the only problem: in 1954 the boathouse was vandalized. Yet this, in the event, resulted in new enthusiasm and might even have been a contributor to the revival of the open regatta.

Despite floods, apathy and poverty, Ironbridge has survived. Four years ago its present boathouse was fitted out; new boats and new blood have had success; the regatta has become a two-day event using a course that, despite cooling-towers, still retains its wooded character; the competitors camp in a landscaped park, and the occasion is one looked forward to by Ironbridge town. Abraham Darby's Coalbrookdale may have been in 1785 a 'scene of superfluous grace, and wasted bloom', according to Anna Seward, 'the Swan of Lichfield', but she certainly could not have savoured the scene at Regatta Meadow.

FURTHER DOWNSTREAM, the town of Bewdley can also boast a rowing club that has existed for over a century. From the early 1880s **Bewdley** RC used a raft moored below the bridge on the Wribbenhall side; at first it was towed to Stourport for the winter but later it remained at Bewdley throughout the year. With changing quarters at one end, landing space at the other, and boat store in the middle, it served the club well until 1933, when during a winter flood the whole structure disappeared. So the arches of the bridge then became the changing-room and boathouse.

The regatta, first held in 1878, was revived in 1930, with the course based initially opposite the present clubhouse but subsequently moved to Halford's Meadow below Dowles Ford.

In the years immediately preceding World War II, construction of the new slipway, and after the hostilities the new clubhouse, boatstore, gymnasium and changing-rooms for men and women, meant that Bewdley began to mark its progress by successes at away venues. Indeed, in one season, 1982, there were over sixty victories.

So, despite floods, this delightful setting has had much to offer club members and visitors at its regattas, even if the thousands of fairylights no longer decorate the bridge.

SITUATED AT THE CONFLUENCE of the River Stour with the Severn, Stourport is the only town directly created as a result of waterways. How appropriate then that rowing should be so important, and the regatta one of the most popular in the country.

The account of the beginning of rowing starts with the Blue Caps. Their four-oar inrigged tub was bought from a solicitor at Bewdley, the town which incidently contributed to Stourport's birth by refusing to have anything to do with the proposed Staffordshire and Worcestershire Canal. This crew was followed by the White Caps, whose most illustrious member was the sculler Broome who beat the Bewdley champion in a race from Stourport to Ribbesford.

However, the real start was with the Red Caps, comprising two foundrymen, a carpenter and a boatbuilder. For two years the Oxford University trainer Timmins brought his eight-oar, standing up in the boat at the regatta wearing his red coat and badge, and the umpire was Salter, the Oxford boatbuilder.

But the regatta had in fact been held before the Red Caps were around. An article in the *Worcester Herald* of 16 September 1864 began thus: 'Lovers of boating had a famous day's amusement at Stourport on Tuesday when there was an inauguration of what will in all probability be an annual regatta ... the course marked out was from Redstone Rock below bridge to a meadow some 450 yards above bridge, making a distance of about a mile and a quarter ... Mr Stephen Salter of Oxford was the umpire, and habited in a scarlet cloak and badge of the Royal Thames National Regatta and mounted on a steed he was quite a conspicuous object as he galloped along the banks to see the starting and ending of the race ... The Chairman (at the end of a subsequent dinner) begged to congratulate the inhabitants of Stourport on having so beautiful a water.'

*Stourport owes its existence to water, and to a canal in particular, for until James Brindley built the Staffordshire and Worcestershire canal in 1766 only an ale-house stood here, and because Bewdley refused to accept the canal this new town was born where the Stour joins the Severn. Today its rowing club enjoys a fine situation by the 1870 bridge, looking across to the town and, more immediately, to the Tontine Inn that was opened by the canal company in 1788.*

Two years later, on 25 August, the *Worcester Journal* repeated the success, reporting: 'This annual regatta took place at Stourport yesterday, several thousand persons attending and lining the banks whilst several contented themselves with a position on the many-arched bridge which spans the stream. The Committee enclosed a small meadow where refreshment and other marquees were erected.'

That bridge was replaced in 1870 by the present iron structure, and six years later the **Stourport** BC was formally established. Its clubhouse stands by the bridge, opposite the Tontine Inn of 1788. If those early Red, White or Blue Caps were to return, the scene at the present-day regatta would not be strange to them, even if there are now outriggers, sliding seats and loudspeakers — and no galloping umpires!

IT IS AT WORCESTER that the Severn attains, as it were, its majority. Here the history of rowing centres on Pitchcroft, that generous floodplain on the north-west side of the city providing a large triangle of green between buildings and river. For over two centuries it has been the scene of horseracing and rowing.

The present **Worcester** RC, itself over a century old, cannot thus claim to be a founding club in the city, yet, together with the King's School, Royal Grammar and College for the Blind clubs, it continues the tradition first established by the Aerial RC in 1841. Before many years had passed, it was joined by such names as Harriet, Nil Desperandum, St George's, Intrepid and Crusaders. These and more have all gone, some because they were too small to survive, some, like the original Worcester RC, for no discernible reason.

The club's first boathouse stood on the present site, behind the racecourse finish, and in about 1900 was replaced by the structure seen today as a relic of the Edwardian age. Somewhat upstaged by the new grandstand, there is nevertheless a continued association between the two sports, for this vast concrete building also contains changing-rooms for the rowing club. New also is the brick boat-store, part of the prestigious River Sports Centre development here.

The result of all this has been seen not only in successes at events

51

*The Pitchcroft lies to the north-west of the city of Worcester but it has been closely associated with racing for centuries. In this drawing it is the water-based kind that has prominence. The view upstream shows the straight almost as far as the Dog and Duck ferry which served as the finish for the old course and the start for the new. In the foreground stands the clubhouse of 1905, its style having an affinity with the pavilion at the cricket ground on New Road. The line of trees is a reminder of the other racing here, for it is the western edge of the racecourse.*

in Britain and on the Continent from junior to veteran level but also in such innovatory projects as the touring and what is termed 'social rowing'.

Worcester has also a rich tradition of regattas. The first recorded was held in 1845. It extended over two days, was midweek and had decorated barges, a ladies' enclosure at the top of the grandstand, a band and significantly no 'intoxicating liquor' on sale.

The course was from Diglis, south of the cathedral, upstream to the Dog and Duck ferry, thus making the boathouse about two-thirds along, though the finish straight allowed good viewing. What was not so good, however, was that that first regatta displayed instances of sharp practice: Bewdley left its station and, despite being bumped by the Oxford (Worcester) club, claimed the prize, refusing to relinquish it to the stewards; two Worcester clubs Unity and Nondescript, matched in a heat were involved in stealing and hiding oars; according to a latter account, there was one sculler who discovered his boat had had a piece of board attached to prevent his winning.

Today the regatta may not be the social occasion of earlier years but the rowing is none the worse; indeed, Worcester may claim to be the venue of more national events outside the Tideway than anywhere else.

*There is much of Worcester's history, both general and rowing, in the left-hand picture. First the general, for not-only does the cathedral feature rightly, but two of the other churches, St Andrew alas now only an elegant 155-foot spire, and the railway bridge for the line that brought so many racegoers to Worcester; and then the rowing, the new boatstore directly ahead and the clubhouse on the left, sharing its premises with the racecourse grandstand.*

*Edgbaston reservoir, Birmingham, has a less majestic rowing base, yet its water is not without history, for it was the great Thomas Telford who constructed the reservoir in 1827 on the site of a medieval coach pond, and subsequent descriptions included such phrases as 'a noble expanse of water'.*

THE EARLIEST KNOWN reference to a rowing club in Birmingham is that to Birmingham Soho Club, which was active in 1859. Like many others in the city during the latter half of the nineteenth century, it was based on the Edgbaston Reservoir, though some used the canals. **Birmingham** RC, dating from 1873, eventually emerged as the sole club in the 1890s and reached a peak of success with victory in the Wyfold Challenge Cup at Henley Royal Regatta in 1904. Then, it seems, a decline set in, and the prospect was grim indeed when, during World War II, the lease of its premises expired and the club lost its presence at the reservoir. Not that the reservoir was a great asset then, for it had been drained to reduce the landmark's value for enemy bombers. To this day a crater can still be seen at 'low water' in September, about a hundred yards from the landing-stage.

In the 1950s new premises became available, though hardly the most attractive, being the former toilets belonging to Billy Butlin's original funfair, sited near the present boathouse. But the club was undeterred, and during the late 1960s an appeal raised sufficient money to build the existing premises. Indeed, the time has now come to consider the next place of expansion, for, since the new boathouse was opened, Birmingham's representation and success at regattas all over the country have steadily increased, so that in recent years the club has produced rowers of international standard.

IT IS AN 'ELYSIAN' field, opposite the Royal Shakespeare Theatre at Stratford-upon-Avon, and it is to be wondered why there was no regatta here until 1874. True the 1860s had seen rowing, but the racing was on a limited scale. The regatta was a great success, showing many of the features associated with that time: a military band, marquees, dancing. So far as racing was concerned, the participants came from local stock, and their pairs, sculls and indeed canoes were all that could be offered.

Yet from this was born the **Stratford-upon-Avon** BC, at a meeting in the Falcon. Despite forecasts of imminent demise, the members soon found themselves the possessors of boathouses, a four, two pairs and two whiffs, with sliding seats too, and most important a location. That was, and still is, beside the Tram Bridge.

For fifteen years or so the club and its regatta flourished, but the

*Stratford-upon-Avon BC has an enviable position for its clubhouse, set beside a park and facing the Shakespeare Memorial Theatre. The drawing was made from the tramway bridge, and the church in the distance is of course Holy Trinity, where Shakespeare rests. It is good to know that the regatta takes in all these, and more, for its start is by Marie Corelli's island, named after the celebrated Edwardian novelist who kept her gondola in a boathouse there. Of this clubhouse in the drawing, its style so admirably characterizes the epithet 'not half timbered'.*

familiar conflict of interest between rowing and pleasure boating gnawed away, to the disadvantage of the former. By 1889 the regatta had succumbed.

However, a change of landlord rekindled enthusiasm: the corporation bought the meadows and gave permission for the erection of a new, much-needed boathouse. Fund-raising, which included the 'Crimson Ramblers' concert party, resulted in a structure costing £404 and looking, in the words of the Club President Sir Arthur Hodgson, like 'something between the Elizabethan and Shakespearian'.

The regatta returned in 1905, with a King's Trophy vase given by the patron, the eccentric novelist Marie Corelli. She characteris-

*Evesham Regatta, founded in 1863, rows upstream on the Avon, its contesting crews using the wide water opposite Abbey Park. With only one bridge to negotiate and another to make for, the course has simplicity, unless the river is in flood. It is a fine setting: as this drawing shows, the Bell Tower, presides, accompanied by the twin spires of All Saints and St Lawrence Churches; in the distance the Workman Bridge carries the London and Oxford road. What more could be wished for, unless it is a return to the use of the Evesham plum boxes as trestles for the boats. Truly it merited the title 'Henley of the Midlands'.*

tically boated, but in a gondola! Until the outbreak of World War I she had considerable influence, on one occasion withdrawing a cup the day after the AGM because it had not been acknowledged.

After the war a golden age of Stratford rowing emerged, interspersed with darker moments, as when on two occasions promising oarsmen were killed in motoring accidents, and lighter episodes, when for instance a spectator dived in to save a 'drowning' man at a life-saving demonstration in the regatta. By 1937 the storm clouds had gathered, the future of the club was in doubt and disaster was averted only by selling the pleasure boats.

The advent of World War II did not mean the end of rowing, for there were RAF oarsmen only too glad to snatch an hour or two from their duties at the nearby training camp. When peace returned, history seemed to repeat itself, with another golden age: 1949 and 1954 were each an *annus mirabilis*.

To catalogue the successes is not the purpose here, but it may be worthwhile mentioning that the club has been in the Olympic trials and has made its mark on the Tideway.

Thus the storms were weathered, the boathouses refurbished and the boats renewed as well as they had ever been. One tradition was established: that of naming them after Shakespeare's heroines, the ceremony being carried out by an actress. Maybe a *Cleopatra* will one day be inscribed: 'The oars were silver, which to the tune of flutes kept stroke'?

'IT IS DESIRABLE to form a club in this town for the cultivation of the art of rowing,' proposed the Reverend W.A. Strong; 'That in connection with this club there be an annual regatta,' added the Reverend T.H. Vines. In such few words **Evesham** RC and regatta came into being on 13 June 1863, at the town hall.

As at Stratford, the potential scene for rowing could not have been better: a generous stretch of lawn, in this case Abbey Park sweeping down to the river, and a generous president, who donated £5, promised an annual £1 and presented the club with its first four-oared boat. A wooden boathouse next to the bridge was built, and all was ready for the regatta a few months later. The course was decided 1½ miles from the bridge to Hampton ferry downstream. By all accounts the event was a great success, not least socially, which may help to explain why in the following year a flower show was incorporated.

In 1876 the river flooded, sweeping away the boathouse and necessitating postponement of the regatta, but by 1890 the new boathouse was to be found on its present site, and the course was amended to upstream from the River Isbourne junction to Evesham Bridge, a distance of three-quarters of a mile.

Honours now began to accrue, and in 1907 the junior four won in eleven out of thirteen regattas entered. The Avon Challenge

Vase was purchased through public subscription, to mark the achievement. Another exceptional year was 1920, and to commemorate the unbeaten record of a crew that won at every regatta both as a four and in pairs, the Vale of Evesham Challenge Trophy, a silver model of the Bell Tower, was cast, again by public subscription.

Floods occurred in 1931 and 1932, when the boathouse was under water and the regatta winners had to be carried on the backs of others to dry land; in another, even more disastrous in 1947 many club records were lost. A loss of a different kind took place in 1966 with the theft of the Challenge Trophy, whilst in the headquarters of the Poplar, Blackwall and District RC.

A Head of the River race was held for some twenty-four years, being replaced in 1975 by a sprint regatta, and in 1984 this was combined with the regatta to make a two-day event.

Such is the reputation of this home of rowing that it has rightly earned the description of 'the Henley of the Midlands'. With names like Crockford, Staite and Thompson, there is no fear for the future, floods or no floods.

Perhaps one regret might be for the passing of the Evesham 'plum boxes', once used as trestles for visitors' boats, but progress cannot be halted!

THE RIVER WYE at Hereford flows straight for some 2,000 metres above the ancient bridge, so it is hardly surprising that such a fine stretch should be the regatta course and that the boathouse of **Hereford** RC is to be found there.

In 1801 rowing competitions between four-oared boats had been held, on a course that began further upstream at Belmont but ended at the Wye Bridge; in 1835 a mile race between three boats also had its finish at the bridge. The next year the length was doubled by adding the return journey to Hunderton, with the prize a £5 purse.

A regatta features first in 1839, and it seems that the contest for a city purse for pairs included at least two boats which had participated in an earlier race for fours. Presumably there were empty seats!

By 1871 the status of the regatta had become such that on the day all the local shops closed, and Earl Somers, Lord Bateman and the mayor gave their patronage. In the junior prize, Hereford's cox was but eight years old.

The next year a newspaper reported that attempts were being made to revive 'the defunct Hereford Rowing Club'. So what had happened, and whether these earlier Hereford crews belonged to the Wye Rowing Club, must remain obscure, particularly as an entry in the *Hereford Journal* of 1862 described the Hereford Club as 'going swimmingly'.

The members of 1896 constructed the original steps down to the river. The old boathouse lasted until 1952, and the new one was officially opened in 1958; most important, the setting is almost unchanged except for the somewhat harsh Greyfriars Bridge. But at least the Old Wye Bridge has been spared and there is now a new vantage-point to view the finishes.

*Hereford Cathedral with the medieval bridge over the Wye in the foreground has been the subject of countless pictures. Here the emphasis is on the 1958 boathouse and the even newer road bridge. It is an enviable stretch of water for the regatta start upstream beyond the railway bridge, with the finish near the boathouse. The gun, incidentally, belongs to the sea cadets' TS 'Antelope'.*

*This drawing of Ross-on-Wye was made while the old wooden boathouse still stood. Its character, so evocative of rowing many years ago, added a pleasant feature to a scene that has such a wealth of beauty. For here the 205-foot slender spire of the parish church, rising behind the Royal Hotel of 1837 standing on the site of the Bishop of Hereford's palace, the pastiche tower and walls so convincing to the eye, the richly varied houses climbing the hill, and the lazy, curving Wye all contribute to the setting that gave Ross the title of 'Henley of the West' during the inter-war years. Even today its regatta is reckoned to be the biggest single-day occasion in the rowing year.*

THE RIVER WYE flows through many beautiful landscapes, and at Ross it seems to find a setting almost perfect. Happily the home of rowing is part of that scene, for the boathouse of **Ross** RC occupies a position that is ideal visually. Whether the old wooden structure of 1908, costing £300 then, contributed to the composition might be debated, but its successor has all the character of a forward-looking club.

Founded before 1874, the club has always attracted support, and its regatta, also over a century old, has invariably been on August Bank Holiday Monday. One programme for 1884 survives, and includes a coracle race. Today it may claim to be the biggest single-day river regatta in the country, and it prides itself on so efficient an organization that, with racing from 9 a.m. to 7.30 p.m., involving some 265 crews, the programme in 1984 overran by only three minutes.

Although the regatta course is a mere 875 yards (800 metres) downstream from the clubhouse, training water does extend for $2\frac{1}{2}$ miles upstream, and it is well used by the impressive fleet of boats.

No wonder Ross was known as 'the Henley of the West' in the 1920s and 30s and it comes as no surprise that over £900 for its new boathouse was raised in two months. John Kyrle, 'the Man of Ross', would have been proud of the club, but then he died 150 years too soon for the regatta.

MANY CLUBS are fortunate in their waters or setting, but **Penarth** RC counts its boathouse as its *pièce de résistance*. True it is shared with the yacht club, but rowing was the original object there, for the earliest document, in 1880, lists 'sailing, rowing in four-oared gigs, sculling, canoeing, swimming, and a duck-hunt'.

The club is to be found on the Esplanade, and it is intriguing to learn that one of the resolutions passed at a meeting of the boat club, as it was then called, requested the secretary to write a letter of complaint to the local board drawing attention to the number of dead animals lying on the beach.

In those early years there seem to have been two phobias: drink and women – that is, until a letter from a woman demanding a ban on drink at the club produced an immediate reaction and the prohibition was rescinded! The other phobia lasted longer, for when in 1895 Constance Vellacot, aged fifteen, entered for the sculls, though of course not a club member, none of the men would compete against her. However, there was a happy sequel: in 1980 she presented the prizes at the regatta.

Four-acred gigs were used in home events and were successful in the Penarth to Barry races of 1896 and 1898. By 1903 outrigged boats were acquired and participation in river regattas became more promising. Nevertheless, stroke did put his foot through the side of one boat at Hereford, about 1930, but a hastily provided substitute gave him an opportunity to redeem himself by winning the heat.

Sixty years ago rowing was forbidden on Sundays, the committee relenting in 1926 'provided the boats were returned to the boathouse by noon, when it was customary for Penarth

*There are not many rowing clubs that occupy architectural treasures, so Penarth is particularly noteworthy in having a Listed Building. It shares the honour with Penarth Yacht Club, of which it is arguably the senior component, since when Penarth boat club was founded in 1880 rowing was the original object. Because it is on the sea front, backed by a steep cliff, the clubhouse can best be appreciated from the beach, and when prizes are presented it is a tight squeeze on the Esplanade.*

residents to take the air on the promenade after church'.

Today the 9¼-mile Penarth to Barry race still takes place, though in 1984 the four was a write off. The regatta still has its hundred-metre (109 yards) course, parallel to the Esplanade. And the Victorian pier still strikes fear into the visiting coxes when they are told they have to steer through it!

CHAPTER SIX

*East*

BEDFORD · CAMBRIDGE · ST NEOTS · ST IVES
PETERBOROUGH · ELY · NORWICH · SUDBURY

ON THE GREAT OUSE at Bedford the most westerly boathouse is
that of the **Star Club**. Formed early in the summer of 1958 by
members of the Royal Air Force Cardington RC, its members were
all service personnel. The reason for Star's creation was to enable
such crews to continue rowing after their discharge. That there was
a need may be seen in the case of the RAF Cardington Eight which
was selected for the British Empire and Commonwealth Games
Trials in 1958: before the games themselves several of the crew
would have become civilians and thus ineligible to represent that
club. Until 1960 it trained and raced under the somewhat
cumbersome title of RAF Cardington and Star Club, having mixed
service and civilian crews.

The RAF Cardington RC had been founded in 1954, rowing
from Bedford School's boathouse at Longholme. Two years later it
moved to a former timber-seasoning shed at Batts Ford, a site once
used by Bedford School, and it shared this rudimentary
accommodation with **Bedford Ladies** RC. In 1960, with the
transition of Star Club, the boathouse was improved by the
addition of changing-rooms.

By the mid 1960s the RAF component had gone, the Silver
Jubilee and, for a time, John Bunyan Schools taking its place.
Strangely, more recently regular servicemen from RAF Henlow
have again become involved. However, 1986 was earmarked for

The Great Ouse at Bedford can justly include itself among the major homes of rowing. As the larger illustration shows, one of the centres is by the Town Bridge where Bedford RC has its boathouse. It is a building with a chequered history, having been the Duck Mill, whose weir is downstream of Monkey Island, then Cheetham's boathouse till 1960, when the rowing club took it over. There are still beams on its façade bearing channels cut by ropes used for lowering the skiffs from the upper floor after Cheetham had built them, despite the restoration that had to be done after a fire in 1984. The elegant classical 1813 bridge spanning the river here was a replacement too, for an earlier structure having a gatehouse on it. Behind the boathouse towers the Moat House, formerly the County Hotel, with St Paul's Church and the Swan Hotel on the opposite bank. The Shire Hall upstream of Town Bridge marks the walk that leads eventually to the subject of the second drawing, the Star Club at Batts Ford. Downstream the boathouses of Bedford Schools may be found. Such is the activity on this water that regattas and Sprints and Heads use the longest possible stretch from Prebend Street Bridge on the west to the suspension bridge downstream, and in both directions too.

demolition of the boathouse, with a new site about a hundred yards downstream designated by the local council.

Regattas are still organized by Star: the Bedford Ladies and Star course is 1,000 metres (two thirds of a mile) starting at the Suspension Bridge and finishing just short of Batts Ford, while the sprint is 500 metres (just under a third of a mile), starting from Bedford RC. They have both become too popular to disappear.

The geographical route from the youngest to the oldest is not easy, but historically the connexion has already been made, for **Bedford School** BC, founded in 1860, originally rowed from Chethams boathouse, which stood on the site of Star Club. In 1922 the present site was used.

Bedford Amateur Regatta began in 1853, and though at first entries by the school were as individuals, by 1866 it was being officially represented. In 1879 the Public Schools fours at Henley attracted Bedford, and the following two it won, perhaps because the school crew greased their seats!

Important as Henley was, the main event of the year for Bedford started in 1895 with its annual race against Shrewsbury School, rowed alternately on the Great Ouse and the Severn.

In 1984 the school produced a coxed four chosen to row for England in the Anglo-French Junior International. It beat not only the two French crews but also St George's representing southern England.

Bedford School is proud of all these successes, but its most treasured memories are of the achievements of Jack Beresford, Old Boy, who was Olympics medallist in 1924, 1928, 1932 and 1936. At the Berlin Games he was presented by Hitler with two small oak trees which he gave to his old school, where they stood until the sports hall was built.

Between Batts Ford and Longholme, the Town Bridge and Monkey Island provide the setting for the third component of Bedford's rowing strength. During the 1880s, as the amateur regatta increased in importance and was included in the calendar for Tideway crews, pressure built up in the town to form a rowing club. As a result in 1886 **Bedford** RC was constituted.

In those early years activity on the Ouse was confined to the summer, but by 1890 the club had recorded its first away win, at Nottingham Regatta, and after ten years most of the Midlands regattas had Bedford representation. Indeed, the club pioneered provincial involvement in the Tideway events.

First mention of winter rowing, with crews out twice a week and evenings, comes in the 1920s. One consequence of this can be seen in the 1922 Bedford Regatta, when the eight was selected only one week before the race, yet won. By 1933 eights were beginning a run of successes culminating in the finals at Henley.

After World War II the all too familiar pattern of meagre funds, antiquated boats, lack of coaches and experienced oars was plaguing the club, yet such was its determination to overcome these handicaps that by 1957 the Silver Goblets and a gold medal at the European Championships came to Bedford members, to be followed by representation for England at home, in Europe and the Olympic Games.

In 1961 the club finally possessed it own premises, after sharing for thirty-four years a boathouse with the Harpur Trust Schools.

Energy was initially diverted into adapting the old boathouse by the Town Bridge into a rowing and social club. The lean years that followed the move nearer the town centre ended in 1968 when Bedford RC again rose to prominence: semi-finalists in the Thames Cup, crews rowing for England in the Home Counties International. Then in the late 1970s junior girls started rowing, one being picked for England. So sound a foundation has enabled this aspect of the club to flourish.

In February 1984 the clubhouse suffered a disaster in physical terms when it caught fire. Yet the resilience and commitment of members have resulted in a better building and increased pride as well as a determination to make the second hundred years even more successful.

One factor that must contribute to this is the younger generation. Before the 1960s it was usual to expect large intakes of ready-made oarsmen from the two main public schools, but this pattern has changed, with members being admitted as raw beginners to be coached *ab initio*. In the next decade efforts were made to attract young people to start rowing at school age; other Bedford schools expressed interest in adding it to their sports syllabus, and pupils were welcomed at the club. From these approaches the Bedford Schools Rowing Association was formed in 1979. Today there are some seventy boys and girls using the facilities of Bedford RC. Their achievements at national and international levels have been outstanding, testimony both to their dedication and to the encouragement given by the club.

THE WINDING RIVER Cam that provides so beautiful a foreground along the Backs has no less an appeal in that part of Cambridge where the homes of rowing can be found.

First then, the boathouses: unlike Oxford's, they happily mix those of town and gown and are all on one side of the river, largely because on the other stretch the spacious Midsummer and Stourbridge Commons, as well as Jesus Green. Like Oxford's they show a variety of styles and ages.

In an order from west to east, the first is Christ's College just before Victoria Avenue Bridge, the **Christ's College** BC having 1830 as its foundation year. Between that bridge and the footbridge

*It requires more than one panorama to include all the homes of rowing at Cambridge, but this drawing's purpose is to show as representative a stretch as is possible amongst such variety. It begins on the left with Fitzwilliam College's, then the spartan Cambridgeshire Rowing Association's single storey, followed by the more elaborate 99 Club's with its clocktower. The two girders standing upright between the last two are all that remain of the century-old wooden structures that were burned down on the night of 31 August 1983. Next comes the City of Cambridge's before the two colleges, Trinity and St Catharine's. As is to be expected, the University's boathouse presents the most sumptuous façade, its multi-paned windows and rich balcony, together with pargeted plasterwork on dormers and gables, reflecting the generosity of its benefactor, Goldie. To end this sequence, the boathouses of Jesus, Trinity Hall and Corpus Christi with Sidney Sussex lead on to Clare, Pembroke and thus to Clare footbridge.*

associated with Fort St George public house is the main cluster of boathouses. The one with scarlet doors belongs to **Lady Margaret** BC, a colour that is forever linked with the strident blazers adopted by college oarsmen in the second half of the nineteenth century. This boatclub is that of St John's College, it being uncertain when the name was officially taken, for the earliest records use 'Johnian

68

BC'. There is little doubt however that the founder of the college, Lady Margaret Beaufort, Mother of Henry VII, had been commemorated on the boats long before 1825 which is the year the LMBC dates itself. Next, parallel to the river is the trim, gabled **Magdalene** and **Queens'**, founded in 1850 and 1830 respectively. **Gonville and Caius** BC, 1827, has its red-brick boathouse standing at an angle to the bank. Incidentally, it was the captain of this club who in 1840 attempted to persuade other captains to ration the champagne their crews allowed themselves on the occasion of the procession of boats, when the eights, decorated with flowers, and the oarsmen in blazers and straws, blades vertical, drank each others' health. The problem was that often there were some thirty boats! **Peterhouse** BC, 1828, brings this group to an end.

After the Fort St George footbridge **Fitzwilliam** BC begins the next sequence, its 'suburban semi' style tricked out in red. The two boathouses which follow are the newest, for on the night of 31 August 1983 their predecessors were consumed in a mighty blaze that can only be generated by the oldest of wooden structures. The **Cambridgeshire Rowing Association** and **Cambridge 99** RC lost much; a few boats were manhandled into the river, but little else. Following the fire, a deliberate act by a city youth, plans were put forward to build one boathouse to house all the 'town' clubs;

69

however, eventually two separate ones were decided upon, and the result can be seen. That of the CRA is spartan and uncompromisingly functional, whereas Cambridge 99 has a 'Swiss cottage'. All that remain as a visible reminder of that dreadful night are a couple of vertical girders standing between the two boathouses. The **City of Cambridge** RC, 1863, escaped the conflagration despite being separated by only a few feet. East of it are the 'modern' façades of white-capped, low-pitched roofs of the **Trinity** BC, 1820, and **St Catharine's** BC, before the opulent elevations of the **Cambridge University** BC, 1827. This boathouse was not of course the original home, dating only from 1882. It owes its magnificence to the munificence of J.H.D. Goldie, a 'Blue' himself. Next to it **Jesus** BC, same year, looks quite homely with its harmonious brown tricks and tiles. **Trinity Hall** BC, 1827, has twin gables and offers hospitality to Homerton College. **Corpus Christi** and **Sidney Sussex** represent the first post World War II design, dating from 1958, followed by **Clare** and **Pembroke**.

The final stretch of boathouses begins at Clare footbridge with **Emmanuel** and **Downing** and continues beyond the Elizabeth Way Bridge to end with the somewhat undistinguished combined boathouses from which a number of clubs row: **Churchill, Selwyn, King's** and the **Leys School**. This length of the river is known as 'the concrete' because of its high concrete bank.

On then to the gasworks, Greendragon Bridge and the railway, which crosses the river just downstream from the finishing-post for the Bumps. Once past the railway bridge, the setting becomes much more rural, with quite sharp bends dividing Long Reach, Plough Reach and Post Reach. A new bridge has been put across the last, to carry the A45. Its position is by the gunsheds where in the bumping races crews line up waiting for the start.

Perhaps the most interesting bend is at Grassy Corner downstream from the Plough Inn, for here the skill of a cox is needed to change over banks, but the spectator may prefer the vantage-point of Church Meadow at Fen Ditton. So far as the town regatta is concerned, the subtle bend outside the Pike and Eel can equally well provide crises, even collisions.

Of course it need hardly be added that the rowing on these

waters is for town and college clubs; the University Eight demand sterner challenges, and their training stretch is downstream at Ely.

FOUNDED IN THIS SMALL market town, **St Neots** RC has provided since 1865 a focus for rowing in the area without a break. From its start the club has used the Great Ouse, though operating from a number of hired sites and buildings. In the mid 1930s a move was made to an Old Mill on the present site, developing it after World War II with a small clubhouse and staging.

A severe gale in January 1976 demolished the boathouse and completely destroyed fifteen craft from eights to sculls, just at a time when the club was constructing a new clubhouse. But generous

*St Neots rowing club has recovered in fine style from the storm which demolished its boathouse in 1976. This drawing shows the impressive riverside frontage it shares, and the regatta field on the nearer bank has the first-rate view of the finish which it has enjoyed since the regatta began in 1865. This stretch of the Ouse is one of the widest throughout its length, providing three lanes for some events.*

*It is the fifteenth-century bridge with its chapel that provides the viewpoint for this drawing. At one time it was also the best place to witness the regatta finish. But even if that is no longer the case, the scene is still worth drawing, for it shows the boathouse of St Ives RC near the tip of the island, as well as the premises of Cambridge University Cruising Club. These buildings may be difficult to pick out, but perhaps that is no bad thing in a waterfront of such harmonious colours; certainly better than being so conspicuous that an aircraft crashes into it, as happened to the spire of the church.*

help from the town, individuals and neighbouring clubs overcame the disaster, so that today there is a well-appointed complex, a comprehensive fleet of boats and excellent stages on a site that makes a major contribution to the riverside amenities of this delightful town.

The club's successes have included the award for the fastest provincial eight in the Tideway Head of 1977 and the gold medal for coxed pairs in the 1980 National Championship, but most important it has produced generations of sound oars adding up to a total of 500 event wins since 1960.

In the year of its formation the club was involved with the regatta and in 1946 took over full responsibility for its organization. By 1978 this had developed into a two-day affair with normal course and sprint events. In early years the presentation prizes took the form of clocks, spoons and similar articles, but today more conventional tankards are given.

These regattas have always been staged from a site on the west bank of the river just north of the main bridge, opposite the club. A two-mile stretch between locks is the normal water for coaching, even though it has no towpath, but for regattas an upstream course with a finish at this Regatta Field just short of the bridge has always been used. Until 1973 the course was generally three-quarters of a mile for Senior crews and scullers with lower status classes using a half mile, but since then it has been established at a thousand metres (two-thirds of a mile) with the sprint a straight 500 metres along the Regatta Field frontage. In 1975 the finishing stretch was widened, enabling three-lane racing in the Invitation Regatta for junior classes in June.

**ST IVES** RC is one of those clubs which modestly declares it has no history, that its boathouse is rather old and tumbledown and its regatta much like any other. Yet many a younger club might well envy the location here, on a frontage that includes buildings of all ages, the Cambridge University Cruising Club almost next door, and an historic stretch of water for its rowing.

The club was formed in 1860, the regatta fourteen years later, and its Small Boats Head in 1982. This last rows a course from Hemingford Lock to the bridge – and what better finish could there be than this?

**WHEN IN** 1981 Peterborough Development Corporation decided to build a bridge for the Eastern Primary Road over the River Nene, **Peterborough City** RC knew that its particular home of rowing would have to move. Since it was formed in 1948, a successor to the old Peterborough RC of ante-1863, the club had enjoyed the fine stretch along the Embankment. Its first premises comprised a large wooden shed, but in 1960 a new boathouse was built, and in the following decades membership expanded, the fleet of boats increased and successes grew to average some twenty trophies each season.

The new home of Peterborough City was to be a mile from the old situated in Nene Park where for seven miles along the river valley could be found a multitude of recreational provision. Through the construction of an embankment and its consequent balancing lake, a thousand-metre course (two-thirds of a mile) with four rowing lanes as well as a double return lane was possible. In 1982 the new boathouse was begun, with the expectation that its

*The two boathouses illustrated on these pages could not be more different in age, style and setting. That on the left is St Ives, over a century old and tucked away in an alley off the Broadway, whereas the larger drawing is of Peterborough's smart new base opened in 1983 at Thorpe Meadows, Nene Park. This prides itself on being designated the East of England Rowing and Canoeing Centre, second only to Holme Pierrepont. It, too, has to wait for the landscape to mature, though one hopes the distant prospect of Peterborough cathedral will survive, but not that of British Sugar Works, fortunately out of the picture.*

facilities would develop to meet the needs of tuition, training and racing.

Here then is a purpose-built water, a worthy partner of Holme Pierrepont, and rich in potential for both. Maybe that new bridge across the river was not such a bad thing after all.

IT IS NOT SURPRISING that the Isle of Ely with its watery context should have a traditional association with rowing. Here the Cambridge University Eight trains, and here too the **King's School Ely** BC has its base.

Records of the boat club date from the 1890s, though until the 1950s rowing was mainly in fours. Its premises used to be at Appleyard and Lincolns Yard, but in the early 1960s the boathouse was built at Babylon, where the marina is now, and access was across the river by ferry until the bridge was constructed in 1965.

Racing at Cambridge regattas and in private fixtures with Cambridge colleges, the Ely theological college and Old Eleans expanded when in 1978 the first eight competed at Henley's Special Race for Schools: since then there have been successes at the National Schools' Regatta and the Schools' Head at Putney.

Now with its new neighbour, the CUBC boathouse, King's looks forward to further activity in what must be one of the most handsome homes of rowing.

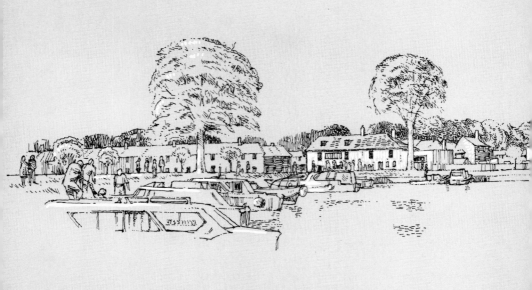

*It is a grand panorama, Babylon at Ely. Here on Waterside the scene takes in, from the right, the maltings of 1868 with its drying-tower, then the superb cathedral, and ends on the left, past The Cutter Inn on the Quai d'orsay, so named because of its twinned town. The marina has moorings for some 200 craft, and its rowing counterpart can be seen to the right at what had been a boatbuilder's yard, Appleyard and Lincoln. Here the newest arrival is the boathouse of Cambridge University, and next to it that of the King's School, Ely. It is to be hoped that neither club returning from practice or race will feel moved to utter the opening of Psalm 137.*

THE RIVER YARE flows through beautiful countryside to the south-east of Norwich. Such a fine stretch of water has naturally attracted rowing of all kinds. It is possible for example to undertake a 27-mile 'marathon' from Oulton Broad at Lowestoft, then Oulton Dyke, down the Waveney, through the Haddiscoe Cut and up the Yare to Norwich.

At present there are three club sites with boathouses serving the city. Along the Whitlingham lane is the Trowse Water Sports Centre, where a former oil-storage depot has become the

clubhouse. Here can be found the boathouses of **Norwich School** BC, originally formed in 1880 and refounded in 1948, and **Norwich** RC, resulting from the amalgamation in 1973 of Yare RC and Norwich ARC, together with the **University of East Anglia** BC, 1966.

The second site is on an island, opposite the King's Head, Thorpe Road, on land owned, appropriately, by a brewery. Here the **Yare** SC has its somewhat quaint headquarters, accessible only by ferry.

A little further along Thorpe Road, down a lane and over a level crossing past the Boat and Bottle, stand the smart new premises of the **Norwich Union** RC. Although inevitably this club has a 'closed' entry, its contribution to rowing in the area has been important since it began in 1905. At first they used Pull's Ferry near the cathedral as a base, but expansion soon demanded other quarters. Just before World War I three of the members sculled to Lowestoft and back, including in their trip a short excursion out to sea! But perhaps the most satisfying achievement was in 1966 when the Wyfold Cup was won at Henley.

On the other hand, cups have been 'lost' at Norwich. Indeed, arguably the oldest rowing trophy in the world, the Carrow Cup,

*Whitlingham Lane leads to the River Yare, where the rowing centre of Norwich may be found, at least the boathouses of Norwich RC and Norwich School BC. But to find Yare BC and Norwich Union RC it would be necessary to cross the river at Thorpe Green, and for the regatta course a longer journey to the site of St Andrew's Church, Whitlingham, with the prospect of the beauties of Surlingham and Bramerton.*

was actually lost by Norwich. It was first awarded for a four-oared race on the Yare from Carrow Bridge to Whitlingham and back in 1813 but disappeared in the 1840s. Strangely, when the Australian Victoria Rowing Association sent a trophy it awarded for a pair-oared race to Britain as a contribution to the 1948 Olympic rowing exhibition, it was recognized as the missing Norfolk trophy! Of course, the characteristic generosity of oarsmen prevailed, and today it is once again awarded by NURC to the winner of a fours race from Pull's Ferry to the Cut. Between times it sits in the Norwich Union vaults.

There are four other events in the racing calendar here: the Norwich Regatta, a 600-metre sprint (just over a third of a mile) the Whitlingham Regatta, the Norfolk Sculls, from Surlingham Ferry to Regatta Finish, and the Head of the River, an event for eights and fours, from Surlingham Bends to Regatta Finish.

For the future, hopes are in the air: there's a plan to create a water park at Bawburgh on the west side of the City, and it could include a thousand-metre (two thirds of a mile) rowing course. Maybe Norwich will not lose this opportunity, remembering how long it took to retrieve the Carrow Cup!

ALTHOUGH EARLY RECORDS have been lost, it is known that **Sudbury** RC, formerly Stour BC, was started in 1873 and restarted ten years later on a credit balance of 12s. 6d. The headquarters had been at Nicholl's boathouse at the Meadow Lane part of the stream, and he sold for £95 two four-oars, one sculler, two canoes and two pair-oars – and spread payment over two years!

A regatta also had been held in 1873, so this was revived too, on a stretch from the old island to the bottom of the reach. August Bank Holiday was chosen, with racing starting at 9.30. Clearly the occasion developed and interested many from the town year by year. A 1904 newspaper stated that, 'The main question that has been agitating the good people of Sudbury for the past week is

*Sudbury RC on the River Stour has a distinguished history and a distinctive neighbour for its boathouse. The building on the right was from 1791 known as 'the great Granary' but in 1981 it became the Quay Theatre, a centre for the arts. On the left-hand side of the drawing the old railway bridge carrying the Sudbury to Cambridge line might represent commerce, while in the centre is the sturdy tower of All Saints whose proudest possession is the heaviest bell in Suffolk.*

whether it will be fine on August Bank Holiday, the day of the annual boat races.' The course now was from the island below Lady's Bridge to Allen's brickyard near the top of the reach. Owing to the narrowness of the river, two winning- and two starting-posts, with a fifty-yard stagger, were used.

Through the 1920s the popularity of the regatta was maintained, even if the station rowing made it difficult to identify winning boats. Perhaps the spectators hoped for repetition of the occasion when the town band, being ferried across the river, ended up in it, instruments included, because the bottom of the punt collapsed.

But in 1931 a greater disaster occurred. Just seven days before the regatta the boathouse was burned, together with all the boats. Banham's of Cambridge, St Ives RC and two Ipswich clubs lent theirs, so the event went ahead. A new boathouse and more up-to-date boats were soon acquired, thus making it the best-equipped club in East Anglia. As a consequence, success attracted many new members, and all seemed set fair. After World War II, age and lack of experience took their toll. Happily, women members now began to make an increasing contribution to the rowing as well as social health of the club.

In 1954 river straightening and widening, after a particularly bad flood, gave the opportunity for a greatly improved course of a thousand metres with a width allowing crews to row abreast. This good fortune was followed by another, when in 1956 the town football club, having purchased Priory Meadow, generously made over the boathouse site free of charge.

All the club now needs is a new boathouse!

CHAPTER SEVEN

*Upper Thames*

OXFORD · RADLEY · ABINGDON · WALLINGFORD
PANGBOURNE · READING

THERE IS NO BETTER place than Godstow at which to start a
description of the Thames at Oxford. The wide, lazy curves sweep
round Port Meadow just below the lock, the Trout Inn, and
remains of the nunnery. Here in 1862 came a memorable boatload
with bow called Dodgson and stroke Duckworth, the cox Alice.
Now the river is more concerned with the practice crews of **St
Edward's School** BC than the narration of a story about a white
rabbit and Wonderland. The boathouse stands at the junction of
tributaries, looking across that wide expanse of Port Meadow to a
panorama of the city beloved by topographers and oarsmen alike.

However, it is at Folly Bridge that the rower's heart begins to
beat. With Salters, established in 1858, the world of boating and
boatbuilding, of skiffs and racing shells opens up. The view
downstream is no longer that of the college barges moored beside
Christ Church Meadow; instead, lined up on the east bank are their
successors the college boathouses. Compared with those at
Cambridge it must be admitted they are undistinguished: there are
no tree-lined greens or commons to set them off, and they are half
the number too. Almost all are shared: the first, **Pembroke**,
founded 1832, with **St Edmund Hall**, 1851; next **Corpus Christi**,
**St John's** and **St Anne's**; an identical design for **Keble** 1870 and
**Jesus**, 1835; then the lower, rather more sleek **Exeter**, 1830, and
**Brasenose**; the dark wood of **Oriel**, 1830, **Lincoln**, 1880, **Queen's**
and **St Hugh's**; **Balliol, New** and **St Benets** repeat Exeter's, the

The centre of Oxford University's rowing is below Folly Bridge, where the majority of the boathouses are grouped. They range to the new cut of the River Cherwell, and their character has less of the variety seen at Cambridge. There is a repetitiveness about them, and the last three are more like banks than boathouses. However, the Isis here is unmistakably rowing water. The two main racing events that take place during the academic year are those, in the Easter Term, known as Torpids, and, in May and June the Summer Eights. Crews race from just above Iffley Lock, and their finish is marked by the posts seen in the drawing on the left where the old confluence with the Cherwell flows under the bridge. On the right, beyond the girder bridge, is the towpath so necessary for training college crews. The university eight uses the river at Henley, or Wallingford before going to the Tideway, as the river here is too narrow, hence the traditional 'bumping' procedure for college races.

Port Meadow upstream of Folly Bridge, at Godstow, is another important home of rowing, for here St Edward's School has its boathouse. The view of Oxford in the distance has been painted innumerable times. But there is a tragic aspect to this place, not unconnected with the activity of rowing, for on the railway line near Port Meadow in 1920 was found the body of Alastair Grahame, son of the author of 'The Wind in the Willows', and indeed it was to him that Kenneth had told that story of the River.

final three in this range virtually identical in their heavy, solid neo-Georgian style more suited to the High Street.

On the opposite, western bank stands the most impressive

*Folly Bridge must be one of the most familiar names to Oxford rowers. This view from the east shows the premises of Salter Brothers, another household word on the water. Established in 1858, the firm soon became not only pleasure craft and steamer-service operators but, more pertinently, builders of camping boats, skiffs and punts, even cabin cruisers and wooden racing shells. On the left is the cut that from 1821 to 1884 had a pound lock, while just beyond the small bridge is Folly House, built in 1849. The main channel is to the right, and over the river stands the former warehouse of 1830, converted in 1975 to the aptly named 'Head of the River'. Trill Mill Stream at its side affords just a glimpse of Christ Church's Tom Tower. Such a description can be no substitute for experiencing the bustle of activity in this area during the summer months.*

*These three drawings illustrate varying aspects of Oxford's rowing scene. The first is of two college barges which used to be moored by Christ Church Meadow. At one time there were twenty-two of them, gorgeous in their exuberance and decoration. However, decay inexorably caught up with them, and they were towed away. But in 1966 a Preservation Trust was formed, setting to work to restore them to their former glory. These two were found near Donnington Bridge, which features in the drawing below of Oxford City RC boathouse. Built in 1971, it is an example of the involvement of 'Town' as well as 'Gown' in the sport. Finally, on the right, the ornate façade of the University boathouse. Built ninety years before the City of Oxford's, it displays its opulence alone on the west bank, surveying its younger companions on the other side of the river with an air of faded superiority.*

boathouse of them all: **Oxford University** BC was formed in 1839, some twelve years after Cambridge's, though it must not be inferred that there had been no organized rowing before then. Indeed, several of the colleges' dates of foundation prove the point.

Nevertheless, with OUBC came quickly races for pairs, fours and sculls, all within two or three years, and most important eights in 1858. This boathouse is not the first; that was built in 1862 in Isis Street above Folly Bridge; nor is it the monopoly of the UBC, for it occupies land leased from University College, and when the reversion came, the club lost its clubroom as well as half its boathouse to the landlord. So this boathouse which looks so large and capacious has to accommodate in fact OUBC, **University College**, 1850, **Wadham, St Peter's**, 1931, **St Catherine's**, 1876, **Linacre**, 1984, and **St Anthony**'s.

Further downstream, at Longbridges, just before that part of the river called the Gut, on the same side stands the last of the college boathouses, Tims, now occupied by **Hertford** 1875, **Mansfield** and **St Hilda's**, 1980. It is not a prepossessing structure, sorely needing a restoration that is being given to some of the old college barges to be seen in a creek opposite.

Finally then to the concrete modernity of Donnington Bridge, where on the eastern bank downstream may be seen the sparkling new boathouse, 1972, of the **City of Oxford** RC. This club was formed in 1968 by the amalgamation of two very much older Oxford clubs, the Neptune RC, founded in 1863, and the Hannington RC, which was the surviving section of a sports club started by the Reverend Dyson in 1905 and named after the great bishop of African fame. Apart from its creditable performances on the water, and enthusiasm in raising funds for the boathouse, acknowledgement must be given to its spirit in taking over responsibility for the Oxford Royal Regatta. First recorded in the middle of last century, this event in the life of the city retained its pre-eminence into the inter-War years. Today it is being revitalized by this club.

Also in Meadow Lane is the **Falcon** RC, established in 1869 and thus the oldest rowing club in Oxford apart from the University's. Falcon originally had NARA affiliation because of its support from local tradesmen, but today it is concerned mainly with social rowing and would like to become a skiff and punting club; it already has a canoe section with internationals in it. Until 1950 there was no boathouse as local hire firms of boatbuilders supplied its needs, but what makes Falcon so unusual is its Dongola Regatta, a fun event paddled in punts with four men and two women, so called from Wolseley's relief expedition to Khartoum when such boats were used to transport troops up the Nile to the province of Dongola.

Further description of the rowing that takes place on this water would be unnecessary, for everyone has heard of the university's course from Iffley Lock to Folly Bridge, of the Torpids in the Easter term, and the Summer Eights at the end of May. Suffice to state that few homes of rowing have such a rich history.

IN 1849, two years after a school was established in William Townsend's early eighteenth-century Radley Hall, boating was introduced there. **Radley College** BC at first used a boathouse downstream from the present site, opposite that of Nuneham. By the early 1860s a move had been made to the weir stream near Sandford Lock, and some fifty years later, in 1911, an extra

*The great house of Nuneham, standing in the park designed by 'Capability' Brown, looks down the steep slope to Radley College's boathouses. They may not be as ornate as Nuneham's, for the 1921 structure was built by Radleians past and present, but their contribution to the development of the college's rowing has been crucial.*

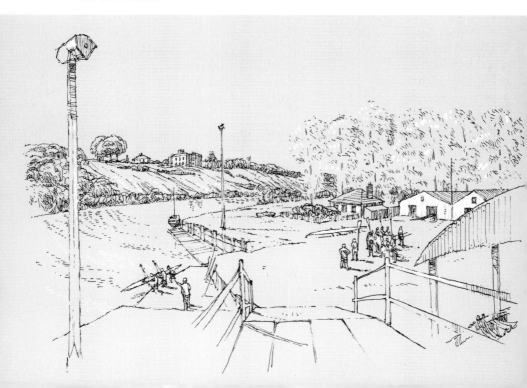

*Abingdon's boathouse is well back from the river, allowing the graceful spire of St Helen's Church to be seen, for the town is at a distance along the Wilsham road. Next to the boathouse a sailing centre helps to create a nucleus of water sport in this beautiful stretch of the Thames.*

boathouse, primarily for the first and second eights, was built near the island in memory of H.M. Evans, who had coached the Radley crews for over a quarter of a century.

Of the two existing boathouses, the older dates from 1921 when, under the supervision of two foremen, masters, boys and Old Radleians built it themselves, and the other from 1966.

The boat club can boast many names important to the sport, Olympic gold and silver medallists, winners of the Double and Diamond Sculls, Goblets, Grand at Henley, not to mention the Prince Philip Cup, but perhaps the most engaging is W.B. Woodgate who, at Henley in 1868, caused confusion and contention by devising a steering that rendered a cox superfluous in the Stewards' Cup. Matters came to a head when the Brasenose College boat contrived its cox doing a 'Jonah' and diving overboard after the start. But there was born out of this the coxless four. Woodgate seems to have been a man for challenges: witness a few years earlier when for a bet he jogged from London to Oxford in some fourteen hours.

DURING THE EARLY 1950s, Abingdon must have been the only town of any size on the Thames not to have had its own rowing club, though evidence of one earlier in the century has been established. The public meeting in 1958 therefore was welcomed by many, and **Abingdon** RC resulted. Formidable problems faced the committee: premises, boats, oars to name but a few. Indeed, the whole enterprise would probably have collapsed there and then but for the generosity of **Abingdon School** BC, founded 1840, which lent from its own resources a pair and clinker IV during the school's summer holiday. During the following winters two twenty-five-year-old fours were bought, and Kettering RC gave an even older boat. Negotiations with the borough led to a lease of land in the Abbey Meadow on which members erected a Nissen hut.

With the first surge of enthusiasm over, the club found the next two years difficult, but in 1961 the Abingdon Head of the River race was started, over a 2,600-metre course (just over one and a half miles) from Sutton Courtenay to St Helen's Wharf, entries coming from places as far apart as Cambridge and Sheffield. New boats were ordered, RAF Abingdon RC shared the boathouse, and affiliation was arranged with the AERE Sports Club – all indications of the club's growth. Then in 1964 trophies started to find their way to the members: Oxford, Pangbourne and Burway, as well as the Oxford City bumping races. Indeed, Abingdon led the way in adopting such modern training systems as weight and circuit exercises.

Then, in 1965, the club had to leave the Abbey Meadow for its new home in Wilsham Road. A year was spent putting up new and permanent premises; improvements were to follow in 1969 and 1983, making the building better suited for the increasing demands of members. Stimulated by this move, the following years saw regatta successes, ladies' rowing and a growing nucleus of enthusiasts.

In 1970 members took part in the National Championship Coxed Pairs, going on to represent Great Britain at the World Youth Championship in Greece. Two years later the crew won a silver medal at Bled. These international successes continued in 1975 at Montreal, and in 1981 the club contributed to the Great Britain Women's Eight in the World Championships, in 1982 the ladies gained places in the National Squad Eight, and men in the Junior Championships in Italy.

Such achievements were in no way diminished by a momentary panic in 1971, when the local council mooted redeveloping the club site as a marina. Although the threat remained for several years, today the prospects are much more settled. Indeed, there is talk of a full-scale regatta, a weekend event, and the Head continues to grow in numbers and classes. Certainly Abingdon has made good on its late start.

IT IS ONE of the attractions of rowing that the finest clubs and the warmest enthusiasms are not necessarily those in the largest cities or with the greatest seniority. **Wallingford** RC could be such an example. This small Thames-side market town, midway between Oxford and Reading, has a population of only 7,000, the club dates only from 1947, and when it was formed there were only three members even moderately skilled at rowing, one with a knowledge of coxing, and twenty-six who had never rowed. Yet the following year's Reading Amateur Regatta saw a crew from Wallingford win

*Wallingford is fortunate in having one of the longest stretches of water on the Upper Thames for rowing. That natural asset is enhanced by its being a particularly attractive town. There are many Georgian houses, interesting churches including St Peter's with its eighteenth-century open work spire like a hypodermic needle acting as a landmark from the river, and intriguing little lanes. Down one of them, Thames Street, stands the Castle Priory malthouse which since 1954 has served as the rowing club's boathouse. Its mellow flint and brickwork harmonizes with neighbouring buildings and, together with the adjacent classical style social club, provides a setting of great charm in an equally charming town.*

the Saunders Challenge Cup, three of the four having started rowing only twelve weeks earlier.

Now, to be quite fair, the club did benefit from the legacy of a town Skiff Regatta that had a committee who generously helped with buying boats, and the Lower Wharf boathouse was made available rent free for a year. Further, when a ballot was held for the only eight sold after the 1948 Olympics, Wallingford drew the winner. So *Portcullis* was purchased for £230 and appeared at Henley in 1957 and 1960.

Soon the club had its own premises, with the help of the **Royal Air Force** RC, 1947; the Castle Priory Malthouse was available in 1953, and by the morning of the 1954 Wallingford Regatta all was ready for its official opening, even though the work of conversion had gone up to 2 a.m. that day. This sharing of the boathouse with the RAF continues to enrich both clubs, and although the service partners may not be so powerful since the end of National Service, men and women rowers from Benson have no doubt about the value of this fine stretch of water on the upper Thames.

Two open competitive events are held here each year: the regatta in May, the first of the major Thames sequence, when the expectation is for around 150 crews from the southern half of the county, and the Long Distance Sculling Head in October.

Wallingford may be small and relatively young but it had five of its members in the 1960 Olympic team; it has won more international medals than possibly any other club, and in 1984 it had forty-five domestic wins. Perhaps, as Colin Porter suggested, it might become the Ratzeburg of Britain — that North German town had only 12,000 population yet produced more world-beating eights than all the other countries put together. But then he would, for he was at Wallingford himself in 1953 and 1954, rowing with the RAF.

COMPETITIVE ROWING on the beautiful stretch of the Thames between Whitchurch and Goring Locks, as it loops through the Gap past spectacular wooded chalk crags, has as its focus the cadets of **Pangbourne College** BC. As befits a nautical foundation, in this case the merchant shipping company Devitt & Moore, the boats comprise not only modern racing shells but also unwieldy gigs directed by a bosun's whistle. Since 1955 the club has been in the forefront of school rowing, with victories at Henley and international honours. It hosts the Oxford Blue Boat Junior International Squads and many other crews eager to savour the challenge of these hazard-free, placid 2,000 metres (roughly a mile and a quarter); indeed, here the National Schools Regatta had its home till 1973.

Upstream the river passes the old Gatehampton Ferry with its white hut, inexplicably known as 'the pink hut' to Pangbournians, then turns sharply at 'Grotto Corner', named after a folly built for the owners of Basildon Park, before the narrow reach of about a mile to Goring.

THERE ARE, or have been, many homes of rowing at Reading. Interestingly, their deployment reflects the dual development of the sport, for here can be seen that dichotomy that bedevilled the early years.

The two reaches of the Thames concerned are those from Mapledurham Lock to Caversham Lock, and Caversham to Sonning Lock. The upper reach boasts five events and three boathouses, the lower one event and two boathouses. To detail then: **Reading** RC, formed in 1867, occupies an upstream site by Caversham Bridge. Its boatstore and clubhouse are due for redevelopment in the next few years, and when that happens there will be a concentration of the school clubs here also. At present **Reading School** BC, 1920, has its premises further upstream on the Thames-side promenade. On the other side of Caversham Bridge and on the opposite bank are the boathouses of **Reading University** BC and WBC, both 1939. Incidentally the **Royal Military Academy, Sandhurst** BC, 1924, used to row from here until it moved to the Reading School BC.

On this upper reach the Reading Amateur Regatta has been held since its inception in 1842, and although it is not enjoying a period of expansion at present, in the 1960s it claimed an importance second only to Henley. Here too, since 1980, are the Sprint Regatta, the Long Distance Sculls from 1965, the Head of the River, 1973, and the Reading University Head, 1935. All have their finish in this favoured setting of public gardens.

*These two drawings of Reading show the homes of rowing each side of Caversham Bridge. The left-hand is of the boathouses downstream belonging to the university: the main building, crisply painted in black and white woodwork, was joined in 1939 by that of the women's rowing club, looking more domestic with its tiled roof. On the other side of the bridge Reading RC has its headquarters. The characterful premises have now reached the end of a useful life, and it is to be hoped that the successor will as admirably fill the space on Thames Side Promenade. Further upstream Reading School has its boathouse, while downstream of Sonning the bases for the town regatta and the Blue Coat School may be found.*

The lower reach has had a very different character. Being near to Huntley & Palmer's biscuit factory, now dismantled, this part of the river was historically used by the Tradesmen's and the Working Men's Rowing Clubs. Consequently their boathouses as well as regattas were here. The Tradesmen's RC was disbanded some twenty years ago, but the Working Men's Regatta lived on, with a change of name to Reading Town Regatta; many say it has increased in popularity and prosperity since then.

Although the former gasworks, the biscuit factory and other manifestations of nineteenth-century Reading, together with the

1940s power-station, have diminished in their visual impact, the resultant pastoral scene by Sonning Meadows may well be short lived, and the regatta's setting could be modified by a new motorway bridge. Most clubs, such as schools' and police, which have begun rowing here tend to move up to the higher reach after a few years. Nevertheless, one remains faithful to its birthplace: **Reading Blue Coat School** BC was formed in 1947, and here it stays at Holme Park, Sonning.

CHAPTER EIGHT

## Middle Thames

HENLEY · MARLOW · MAIDENHEAD · ETON
LALEHAM · WEYBRIDGE · KINGSTON

HENLEY – THE NAME of this small Oxfordshire town is to many
people synonymous with rowing, possibly the only regatta they
think still held. It conjures up in the imagination all the features
associated with Edwardian leisure, the faded photographs of a
crowded river, parasols and picture hats. This is the ideal all other
regattas aspired to, the one by which they are compared, whether
in age or size or that more visual ambience of marquees, enclosures,
lawns and fluttering bunting. Gone are the regattas where the
whole town was *en fête*, where the band played and the firework
display brought a day of crowded excitement to an end – except at
Henley. Of course, it is possible to sneer: the ridiculous faded
rowing cap sitting on the bald head, the absurdities of blazers
out-colouring the gaudiest of summer dresses, the strident accents,
the seeming casualness of interest in rowing. Yet Henley continues
year by year, the paragon of regattas, the goal of every oarsmen.

Others have written on the history of the racing, listing winners
of Diamond Sculls, Stewards' Challenge, Silver Goblets, Wyfolds
and Visitors till almost every name known to the sport appears
somewhere; the technical developments too have their chroniclers,
keel-less eights, outriggers, sliding seats, and so on; then there are
those who have detailed the changes in organization, professional
and amateur, coxes and coxless, staggered starts, heats and stations;
some write of the social side, visits by monarchs, celebrities,
fashions and *faux-pas*. But here let the focus be on the water.

94

*Leander Club has a permanent presence at Henley, for its substantial premises are there when the tents and stands have gone. This drawing illustrates its interior during the Henley Royal, with the busy throng of visitors and members. Above the doorway can be seen the end of the boat which won the Grand Challenge Cup in 1898, 1899 and 1900, while in the case above the pigeonholes is a scale model of the first keelless racing four of 1854, winner of the Stewards and Wyfold Cups the following year. What this drawing cannot show is the pink decoration, a distinctive characteristic of Leander. The roof of the boat tent is seen through the right-hand door. For many years the Regatta headquarters were here, but a new building on the other side of the bridge, where the Carpenters Arms stood, was begun in 1985. This structure was designed to accommodate not only staff but also the sixty-foot timbers when they are not acting as the booms for the racing.*

It was the $2\frac{1}{4}$-mile stretch from Hambledon Lock to Henley Bridge that started it all, when on 10 June 1829 the crews of Oxford and Cambridge rowed their first boat race here. After a collision at

Temple Island, the second attempt resulted in a win for Oxford. The really important result though, so far as Henley was concerned, was that some 20,000 spectators watched. That evening's event, which included a firework display, was but the overture to a long-running performance. There were further races on Henley

*Henley's Royal Regatta must be one of the most familiar events in the rowing calendar, and this view looking upstream to the finish of the course the subject of countless pictures, yet its attractiveness does not diminish with the changing years. At one time the rowing lanes would have been surrounded by spectators boats; today the pleasure traffic is kept well clear by the booms whose upright posts are so conspicuous. What has not changed is the tented Stewards' Enclosure. In this drawing a little licence has been taken to permit inclusion of the bridge, the Angel and Red Lion hotels as well as the floating grandstand, though in reality it is the tower of St Mary's Church which aligns with the course. The range of gables begins with those of the Little White Hart and continues to the right with the boathouses' ornate quintet. Further along the bank the trees mark the presence of Phyllis Court.*

Reach: Leander in 1831 took on Oxford Amateurs over the same course and won; Lady Margaret BC, Cambridge, lost to the Queen's College, Oxford, in 1837 over 2½ miles (another boat race in 1836 had settled on Westminster to Putney despite Oxford's preference for Henley or Maidenhead) but in 1839 the regatta was born.

A meeting at Henley town hall decided that an annual regatta would produce benefits for the town, the neighbourhood and the public in general. The course was fixed at a distance beginning at Temple Island and ending by the bridge, the umpire to officiate by accompanying each race on horseback. Despite an inauspicious start, with one of those mighty Thames thunderstorms, the weather had cleared by the afternoon, allowing the spectators in their thousands to occupy not only the customary bridge but also both banks and specially erected stands. The bells of St Mary's rang out, cannon fired and music from two bands provided an aural background. Thus a pattern was set that has not changed greatly over the years.

Inevitably there have been other kinds of change. For one thing it became royal, when Prince Albert gave it his patronage in the year

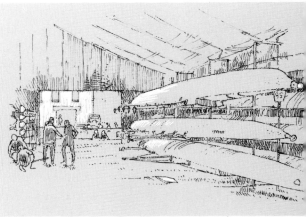

*Henley Bridge, built in 1786 to replace a timber structure itself a successor to a stone one, is not only a feature of the regattas, when it affords a fine view of the colourful scene, but also a design of some elegance and interest in its own right. The centre arches have carved keystones representing Thames and Isis, the work of Anne Seymour Damer, to whom Horace Walpole bequeathed his Gothick house, Strawberry Hill at Twickenham.*

*The other subject of these drawings is the interior of the spacious boat tent that occupies so much of the area between the Enclosure and Leander during the Royal Regatta. A walk round its aisles makes for an education in identifying club colours and insignia.*

of the Great Exhibition, 1851. Then 1885 saw the stewards opening their ranks to include rowing as well as local personalities, at the same time constituting a committee to run the regatta. On the Berkshire side of the reach the inlets and bays were piled, to prevent crews going into the slack. The following year a change was made in the course, moving the start to below Temple Island and giving boats three lanes. By 1879 the width had been reduced by 30 feet to 120 feet at the start and 110 at the finish. Furthermore the starts were staggered, so that no advantage came to any station because of the minor bends. In 1891 the practice of lining sterns for the start and deciding by bows for the finish, which had led to unfairness if boats varied in length, was amended. Till 1906 the umpire also acted as timekeeper, but at least that was an improvement on the procedure in the early years when the start was observed from the stewards' stand through telescope, a flag signal made across the river to Lion Meadow where a signal gun was fired to begin the timing.

By 1886 the Buckinghamshire bank was similarly piled off. But this did nothing to reduce the increasing congestion on the reach, for on the course from Phyllis Court to Temple Island would be found houseboats, launches and myriads of smaller craft. Indeed, there was an incident the following year, at the Jubilee Regatta, when a sculler, a hundred yards before the finish, crashed into the boats of a royal party including the Princess of Wales. His boat and sculls were broken, but there was no offer to re-row the race. In this year too the finishing-line was moved to Poplar Point, to avoid the bend, and by 1924 the present straight course, the result of excavation of the Berkshire Bank and part of Temple Island, eighty feet wide and one mile 550 yards long, had been introduced. Inevitably this has meant that only two crews can row abreast, and *repêchage* is out of the question. But at least there has been the introduction of booms to keep the course clear, even if they have to be reset each year.

Timings for this stretch are now based on Remenham Barrier, originally the first horse-gate across the towpath, 2,089 feet from the start; Fawley at 3,435 feet, and the winning-post at 6,930.

For many years the regatta office has been on the south end of Leander Club, but with the erection in 1985 of a new headquarters building on the other side of the bridge, where the Carpenters Arms used to be, there has come a new phase in the history of Henley Royal.

This physical moving is an experience **Leander** has had itself a number of times in its life. From the available records, the club was in existence by 1818, its name almost certainly from one of the professional watermen's boats that the gentlemen rowers would hire, the charges on its shield of star and arrow being similarly derived. In the 1820s this small group boated from Bishop's yard, at Stangate; in the 30s its clubroom was at Searle's boathouse in Lambeth. When Henley's Regatta began, Leander decided not to compete, despite its association with compiling the rules and, incidentally, a member acting as the regatta's first umpire. But it came to look, rowing through that stormy morning from London.

By 1840 it was fully participating, winning the Grand Challenge Cup. In 1866 it had its first boathouse, at Putney, and although this building was not relinquished till 1939, increasing involvement at Henley saw it initially renting a clubroom at the Royal Hotel, then an enclosure on Temple Island, and finally in 1895 building the substantial clubhouse. Interestingly, Phyllis Court became available for purchase soon afterwards, but, like the regatta stewards, Leander decided against its acquisition. For a time the enclosure was moved down to the field below the White House next to the Remenham Club.

Records of Leander's rowing successes at Henley and elsewhere must be for others to recite; suffice to state that its role in the regatta scene is unassailable, its pink unmistakable and its clubhouse incomparable. One further point may be made: surmounting its shield Leander's crest is a hippotamus. The jibe that it is the only

*Temple Island, 2,100 metres or 1 mile $\frac{2}{3}$ furlongs from the finish of the Royal Regatta, Henley, has always been associated with the racing. Although the start of the course has varied, this feature, clearly seen from the enclosures, has made its visual contribution to the wonderfully straight stretch of water. At one time Leander's enclosure, it was built by James Wyatt in 1771.*

*Important as the Henley Royal is, there is other rowing from this town. Indeed, Henley RC was founded the same year as the Royal, 1839, and its boathouse, illustrated here, has a fine location opposite the boat tent and pontoons during the Week.*

aquatic creature, apart from a Leander member, which keeps its nose permanently in the air, can surely be true no longer.

Palatial as Leander's clubhouse may be, it must concede that the boathouse of **Upper Thames** RC has one distinction over it. This club, formed in 1962, is the only one actually sited on the regatta course, next to the Remenham. Such an opportunity to train on this reach is not to be missed, and consequently over the past twenty-four years oars from clubs, schools and universities from all parts of this country and the rest of the world have been given hospitality here. Not only that: the club holds a fours and small boats Head, while **King James's College** BC, which also boats from here, has a junior eights and fours Head.

But the rowing riches of this town are not exhausted yet, for there is also **Henley** RC. Its boathouse, humbly set by the Little White Hart on the opposite bank to Leander, has a charm of its own. It comes into its own too at the Town and Visitors Regatta, the fours and scullers Heads, for this club can claim to be, in age at least the equal of the Henley Royal Regatta: its year of formation, 1839.

THE VIEWS of Jerome K. Jerome, author of *Three Men in a Boat*, on rowing may not be worth very much, but his opinion of Marlow, 'one of the pleasantest river centres I know of', will be confirmed by those who have visited it. The group of church, bridge and river is well known through countless calendars and travel guides, but what is less obvious is that the spot from which to see it is by the boathouse of **Marlow** RC.

It is almost certain that Marlow had rowing before the club was formed in 1871, if only because of a poster, still treasured by the members, advertising a regatta in 1855. By the late 70s it had become a regular occasion, taking place since just after the end of World War I at the end of the third week in June, ten days before Henley. Because this timing offers valuable experience for the Royal Regatta, entries have been large, and twenty races are a normal programme. Crews are able to row three abreast, thanks to the generous width of the river. Many countries have been represented, giving it the character of an international regatta. Until 1968 the course was seven furlongs, but in that year it was lengthened to a mile, the start being at Temple Mills and the finish opposite the enclosure in Higginson Park.

The boathouse is a mixture of late Victorian and modern, having been opened in 1897, then extended in 1973. From here crews have travelled to one or more of the Thames regattas every year since the club was founded. And in 1919 the boathouse and boats were put at the disposal of the ladies of Newnham College, Cambridge, and the London School of Medicine for Women, when the first eights race on the Thames took place. Little wonder that since 1919 Marlow RC has welcomed women as active members.

*It is a frequent experience to find the boathouses of rowing clubs close to a bridge, and these two drawings confirm it. The first, of Marlow, shows the interesting detail of Tierney Clark's only surviving bridge (his Hammersmith design was superseded, and Budapest's destroyed in World War II). The second, Maidenhead, had Sir Robert Taylor as its designer in 1772. The boathouse once served as a cushion store for a pleasure-boating firm. Here the regatta is held on the reach below Brunel's railway bridge of 1837, another structure of some historic importance for it has the widest brick-built span anywhere. There is even a belief that it was the subject of Turner's famous painting 'Rain, Steam and Speed'.*

 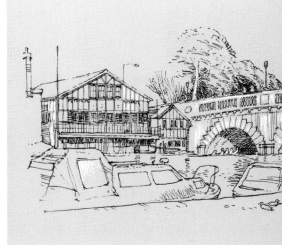

*The church and bridge at Marlow make a fine composition. Although both are nineteenth century, there are few settings for a regatta finish to better this. Over the river from the boathouse by the bridge, Higginson Park, to the left of the new buildings, accommodates the enclosure and boat area. The suspension bridge itself, designed by William Tierney Clark in 1831, has a splendid view downstream to the weir, as well as upstream to Bisham Abbey and Temple Mills, where the regatta course starts. Interestingly, the wrought iron crossbeams of 1860 replace the old wooden ones and bear on their ends the medallion of the seal of the Chiltern Hundred of Desborough from which the famous Lord Desborough, Chairman of the Thames Conservancy Board, took his title. It was here at Marlow that the first women's eights raced in 1919, and the rowing club lent both boats and boathouse.*

**MAIDENHEAD** RC, founded in 1876, has always had its headquarters too by the bridge. The present men's changing-room was its original premises, for the boathouse and ballroom above were then a cushion store for Bond's boathouse. But even if the accommodation is small for today's needs, it has not limited the club's achievements. At Henley the Thames, Wyfold, Queen Mother and Britannia Cups have all come to Maidenhead; at the 1948 Olympics the club provided half the winning crew in the double sculls.

In its own water, the regatta, begun in 1893 as an independent concern, has since the late 1970s been part of the club's responsibility. The course, originally 1,100 metres (about two-thirds of a mile), is now 800 metres (about half a mile), to make for fairer rowing and sharing with other river-users. Its location is the reach below Brunel's railway bridge, which has incidentally the longest brick-built span in the world. Not only has the club taken over this regatta but it has also benefited from another, Bourne End, whose Challenge Cups on its demise passed to Maidenhead.

EVERYBODY KNOWS of the Eton boating song, even if the words are not so familiar: 'Jolly boating weather' and 'blade on the feather' together with mention of 'hay harvest breeze' and 'swing, swing together, with your bodies between your knees'. It was written in 1865, some seventy-two years after the first organized regatta, while the **Eton College** BC dates its foundation from 1816.

The origins of the use of the river here for sport and recreation took the form of organizing crews in imitation of Nelson's Navy, with boats being given such names as *Dreadnought*, *The Majestic*, *Defiance* and *Britannia*. Expeditions were made upstream, one annual trip being to Boveney, where a Mr Townley Ward, at 'The Willows', which was dubbed 'Surly Hall', gave supper. Another event was the Procession of Boats on 4 June to celebrate George III's birthday, and 'Election Saturday' provided an occasion too for going to the river. Not surprisingly, these outings presented opportunities for challenges, and racing, often of the bumping kind, resulted on the way back.

Soon challenges were going out to others, notably to Westminster School in 1818 and 1820, but the headmaster forbade his boys to participate. Indeed, it was not until 1840 that rowing was officially recognized at Eton. The college's subsequent successes at Henley, where it first competed in 1861, its seven consecutive

*The bridge, now for pedestrians only, that spans the river between Windsor and Eton is the viewpoint for this illustration of Rafts. It is the main boathouse for Eton College, and its complicated range of buildings bears witness to the considerable changes that have taken place here over the years. Even today it embraces not only the schools rowing, under the term Eton College Boat House Ltd, but also the boatbuilding firm of Matt Wood.*

wins in the Ladies Plate in a total of twenty-two before World War I, the more recent Princess Elizabeth Challenge Cup, and its problems of examinations conflicting with the regatta date: all these are chronicled elsewhere. Similarly the growth of school rowing to include under-fifteen and under-sixteen age groups, second and third eights, with greater competitive use of fours and pairs; the increasing involvement in international rowing (there are only three years since 1967 that Etonians have not been in British teams at the junior regattas), not forgetting the former Etonians who have been Olympics medallists – all these are but indications of the important contribution this royal college has made to rowing.

The Thames dividing Eton from Windsor flows in an S-bend from the Brocas to the railway bridge downstream. Above Boveney Lock is Andrew's boathouse, constructed some twenty or thirty

*Eton's second boathouse is Masters', downstream from Fellows'*
*Eyot where the Procession of Boats takes place. From it there is*
*a fine view of the Thames as it sweeps round what is known as*
*the Triangle, with the college chapel behind. The panorama*
*takes in Windsor Castle too, but the best prospect for this is at*
*the end of Rafts on the Brocas, as the left drawing shows.*
*Incidentally, there is a third Eton College boathouse, called*
*Andrews, upriver on the way to Dorney.*

years ago, and just before the railway bridge, Masters', from
which the view looking upstream to the College Chapel is most
memorable. But it is the third of Eton's boathouses which has the
greatest historical interest.

At the eastern end of the Brocas is a piece of land originally
owned by the family of that name, from Beaurepaire in France, and
sold to the Provost of Eton in the fifteenth century. Rafts is a
complex of buildings adjacent to Windsor footbridge. In 1847
Roger Tolladay sold his boathouse to Searle, who in 1870 sold it to
Salter; meanwhile next door William Goodman took over Hester's

boatsheds. By 1875 Parkins was running Salter's, and ten years later Goodman had given place to Winter. This complicated sequence resolved itself into the Brocas Boat House Company, then in 1910 as Eton College Boat House. Repairs, restoration and reconstruction of the buildings have all helped to modify the waterside scene, so that today the Company, run by masters and boys, sharing its site with the famous firm of Matt Wood, makes a splendidly varied frontage.

Off the Brocas near Rafts was the original location for the Procession of Boats, with its ten-car *Monarch* echoing the royal barge. In recent times there has been a move downstream to the reach at Fellows' Eyot; it takes place in the afternoon now, and sadly the firework display has ceased. But though such changes have come, the boating song still promises, 'We'll row for ever, steady from stroke to bow' – even if the Ladies' Plate at Henley in 1960 was won with fixed pins long after other people had abandoned them!

FORTUNATE IS THE CLUB that has enjoyed a permanent home and

name; those not so lucky have sometimes wondered if they were for ever to be nomadic. **Burway** RC was founded in 1921 as Staines Town BC. Its first home was near Bell Weir Lock at Runnymede, but then it moved to Laleham Reach, Chertsey, and its name changed to Burway RC, after the island on which the clubhouse stood. However, in 1979, because of an increase in the rental which it could not afford to pay, the club was obliged to leave these premises. Whilst a new site was being prepared and a building erected at Laleham Park, on the opposite side of the river, many months were spent as the guests of **Strodes College** BC, Egham.

Eventually, in April 1981, the new boathouse was ready and the opening ceremony took place that autumn. Now the club was able to devote its energies fully to rowing, particularly organizing the two Head of the River races, one for eights and fours held in

*Burway RC at Laleham is not easy to find, but once busy main roads have been left behind, Thameside is a quiet stretch of water, spacious with its grass and trees. Rowing here is very different from that at nearby Thorpe Park, though both places have their contribution to make.*

February since 1953, the other for smaller boats, since 1980 held in December. Both use a course 3,000 metres (almost two miles) upstream between Chertsey and Penton Hook locks, which demands tactical judgement particularly in the matter of bends, for there are several in each direction, and if crews do not take the correct line into them, they may well find themselves on the outside when overtaking slower boats.

But Burway should have no problems itself, for among its members two have rowed for the Moscow Olympics, one at Los Angeles, the club secretary was for five years coach to the Women's Junior National Squad, and last but not least a recent Director of Coaching at the ARA was brought up on this stretch of water.

THE EMERGENCE of women's rowing can be no better illustrated than at Weybridge on the Thames. Starting in 1919, the involvement of women here owed much to the parent club, Weybridge RC, when opportunities were made for training four women's fours. A women's section was formed, resulting five years later in a crew being invited to a charity regatta in Brussels where success was crowned by their being presented to Albert, King of the Belgians.

Such propitious beginnings led almost immediately, in 1926, to the foundation of the **Weybridge Ladies** ARC. In the first women's eight race over the university course from Putney to Mortlake, the club won. This achievement was matched by further successes at home and abroad during the 1930s, not the least being those of founder member and captain Amy Gentry, who in 1939 became chairman of the Women's ARA. Through the generosity of the club's president, Lady May, a boathouse was made available in 1932, and when it was put on the market in 1946, Amy's father bought it for the club. In 1950 Amy herself came out of retirement to stroke the senior crew successfully at three regattas on the Thames.

Year after year the club has achieved glory: in the Tideway Head, at the National Championships, in the National Women's Squad at the Olympics, and in the World Junior Championships. Weybridge ladies have been fortunate in their benefactors, but they certainly have not rested on their oars.

So far as **Weybridge** RC itself is concerned, the club was founded in 1880, and its boathouse erected during the first decade of the present century. Based on an island owned by the National Trust, on an attractive stretch of the Thames, little wonder that the rowing has been both rich and varied. In 1922 the club began the Weybridge Regatta, while its successes nationally continued to accumulate. In 1984 lady members were admitted, at last!

IT IS SURPRISING that Kingston, as a town of markets, boathouses and two excellent schools, the grammar and Tiffin, admirably suited for the foundation of a rowing club, had to wait until 1858 for one. The weatherboarded Messengers boathouse on Ravens Ait was the **Kingston** RC's first premises, and within four years the club had won the Wyfolds at Henley. However, three years later

*Kingston-upon-Thames rowing has its base at Hampton Wick. The boathouse in Canbury Gardens was built in 1968, but since then the view across the river has changed greatly, with new tower blocks. However, some features remain, not least being the delightful private boathouses belonging to houses now gone. At one time the regatta took place at Stevens Ait further upstream, but today the finish is at Canbury Gardens. In the drawing, done from inside the clubhouse, the presence of pennants and insignia is worth comment, for this practice of displaying honours as well as past records and photographs of crews is to be commended.*

the stewards instituted the 'Kingston Law' requiring crews to have at least two months membership of their club; perhaps Kingston had been 'packing' with college oars? In 1868 the Wyfolds was again won, through the opponents, Brasenose, jettisoning their cox.

Kingston has always been involved with the organization of Thames rowing: in 1879 it was instrumental in forming the Amateur Rowing Association out of the Old Metropolitan, in 1903 it helped the birth of the Thames Amateur Rowing Council, and in 1909 it was one of the seven founding members of the Remenham Club at Henley.

Meanwhile successes were being won: Wingfields, Wyfolds, Thames. The name of W.B. Woodgate occurs with regularity – he was associated with the club for fifty-eight years. Another member, and captain, was R.C. Sherriff, who in fact wrote his ever-popular play *Journey's End* for the benefit of the club.

In 1935, when the rental for the premises became too great, the move to Albany boathouse in Kingston was decided upon. However, bigger and better headquarters were needed with an increasing membership in the 1950s, and the happy outcome was the Canbury Gardens site. Here the borough council designated a waterside plot and, joining forces with **Tiffin School** BC, which had been started in 1890, the club came into possession of a new boathouse overlooking one of the best stretches of upstream Thames.

The Kingston Amateur Regatta also appreciates this reach, for since 1855 it has been held here. Starting at the downstream end of Stevens Ait, its present course ends 600 metres (just over a third of a mile) up river at Canbury Gardens. Then there is the Sprint Regatta, and since 1959 the Head of the River, from Hampton Court to Teddington, together with a Small Boats Head.

CHAPTER NINE


*Thames Tideway*

PUTNEY · HAMMERSMITH · CHISWICK
BRENTFORD · TWICKENHAM

AFTER TWICKENHAM, the sweeping curves of the River Thames create a gigantic 'S' from Chiswick and Mortlake to Putney and Fulham. Such a stretch, with its ebb and flow, its dramatic changes of level, its notable bridges and a riverside rich in history, has been the setting for rowing over centuries. Since 1845 it has seen the annual Oxford and Cambridge Boat Race, since 1926 the Head of the River Race. Here the Wingfield Sculls have been competed for, beginning in 1830; the Scullers' Head was established in 1954. Then there are the women's events and the regattas, while in 1982 the ARA centenary pageant could not but start from Putney, even if it did continue downstream.

Threading this course, like beads, are the rowing clubs whose names alone create an oarsman's almanac. They dispose themselves roughly into three clusters, at Putney, Hammersmith and Chiswick, with one or two dispersed between.

THE BOATHOUSES at Putney are on the upstream side of the bridge ranged along an embankment constructed in 1887, and the sequence begins appropriately enough with the senior club. In 1856 Josias Nottidge, a leading oarsman of Putney, called a meeting to form a rowing club which would not peter out as many had been doing on the Tideway. So his proposal was to encourage a large number of members 'having at heart the interest of aquatic sports' paying a

*The downstream end of what is known as the Tideway is at Putney. Here, ranged along the slipway, boathouses stand shoulder to shoulder, their names a rollcall of rowing. In this drawing London RC features most prominently, its massive brick façade echoed by the cast-iron base of its flagstaff and the bollards which demarcate frontages. Then follow the headquarters of school, college, bank and club, each seemingly with its own balcony, slipway and flagstaff. In the distance beyond the curve of the river at Barn Elms the bold skyline of Harrod's repository can be seen, and on the north bank the floodlights for Fulham football ground.*

small annual subscription. This, he felt, would ensure survival and at the same time arrest the increasing dominance of the steamboat. It was necessary to stop this 'decadence of a manly and healthy sport', where the flashing oars of a London eight seemed 'rapidly becoming a thing of the past'. Thus the **London** RC was born, clubrooms were specially constructed at the Star and Garter, on the Putney Embankment, and a boathouse was built some 200 yards upstream; membership numbered 140, with the optimistic expectation of doubling it soon.

*One oddity at Putney is the Duke's Head on the Embankment for it is a reminder that in the nineteenth century many rowing clubs were based at public houses. But in this case the actual boathouse is here, and perhaps it represents the only instance of such an arrangement today. Putney Town RC must welcome so happy a conjunction of exertion and refreshment.*

*Such names as Fulham, Harrod's and Barn Elms have become familiar through commentaries of the University Boat Race. This second drawing shows where the start is marked by the stone. Across the river, Fulham church borders the park of Fulham Palace, once the residence of the bishops of London.*

Five members, including Nottidge, entered for Henley that first year, ostensibly from the Argonauts BC to satisfy the one year's existence qualification, winning the Stewards, Wyfold Fours, Goblets and Diamonds! A name which occurred in all these successes was Alexander Alcee Casamajor's, one of the first scullers of his day.

It is interesting to note the club ordered, apart from eights and fours, a twelve-oared outrigger which proved so popular that another was made. Races between the two became regular events, and on occasion their services were employed in pacing the University crews during training.

By the end of the 1860s the clubrooms at the Star and Garter had become insufficient, so it was decided to build a combined boat-and clubhouse on the existing boathouse site. That structure, opened in 1871, extended in 1875 and 1884, restored ninety years later, must be one of the finest any club could wish for. In it is a room named after Steve Fairbairn, who in 1926 came to coach. Fortune smiled on LRC, even though he stayed only two years. In the following decade, such was his influence, the Grand, the Stewards, Wyfolds, Goblets, the Wingfield and the Tideway Head were among the proliferating successes.

Indeed, 1932 was accounted a year of defeat because, though the Thames Cup and the Wyfolds had been won together with many up-river trophies, the Grand was missing! The following year therefore the first eight won not only the Grand but also every other event entered. It almost goes without saying that the club achieved international representation: Olympics, including two gold medals at one regatta, Empire Games, FISA Championships – the list is long.

Yet perhaps the club's greatest contribution to Tideway rowing lay not in its own honours but in the part it played in helping to establish the Metropolitan Amateur Regatta. Following the proposal for a Procession of Boats on the Tideway, the Committee of Metropolitan Rowing Clubs appointed the Captain of London RC as chairman, and another member, Charles Dickens' son, as secretary, to head a committee charged with organizing 'a really grand National Regatta, which it is expected will prove a great attraction to all rowing men'. The first year, 1866, justified that hope, and indeed it soon rivalled Henley. But the euphoria dissolved: complaints arose regarding clubs not paying their share of the expense. Consequently responsibility for running the whole event was shouldered by London RC, and over the ensuing century its fortunes fluctuated. Variations in form were tried, the length set at a mile and a quarter (2,000 metres) and finally, in an attempt to attract more public interest, it was held on a Sunday. However, by 1977 there were clear indications that a move would have to be made, especially as a regatta on tidal water was inappropriate for those oarsmen accustomed to still waters with multi-lane courses. So in 1980 the 'Met' was held at Thorpe Park, Chertsey, but the London RC can be proud of its contribution to the history of the regatta, the first in the Thames Valley to have multi-lane racing.

Established in 1922, like many clubs the partial result of post-war relaxation and extensions of recreational facilities, **Putney Town** RC is possibly unique in rowing from a public house. The Duke's Head has been the home for a club that has welcomed as members many oarsmen who were not able to join the other Tideway clubs, and its founding eleven years after the successful inauguration of Putney Town Regatta, under the auspices of the Tradesmen's Rowing Association, was significant.

In this group on Putney Embankment there are also the boathouses used by a number of banks: the **National Westminster Bank** RC was formed in 1968 from an amalgamation of two much older clubs, the National Provincial of 1884 and the Westminster 1906; **Barclays Bank** RC dates from 1936; while the **Midland Bank** RC, founded in 1878, moved here from Hammersmith in 1926, during the captaincy of one of its most illustrious members, T.D.A. Collet, who rowed for Cambridge three years in succession and won a bronze medal in the single sculls at the 1928 Olympics.

Here too is the boathouse of **Westminster School** BC, a school whose history of rowing must be one of the longest anywhere, for it existed before the founding of Leander (which incidentally once had its headquarters at Putney) and the start of college rowing at Oxford. Strange then that in 1867 the school could not muster enough boys fit to crew, that in 1884 a headmaster introduced a timetable that made it impossible to find the time to row, that earlier, in 1820, another head forbade a race with Eton and that again, in 1894, the interdict was applied to King's Scholars. Yet in 1837 the sport had received royal approval, when William IV invited the crew to Windsor before the Eton race, though it was later put about that he only did it to upset them! It did not work, for Eton lost.

**Lensbury** RC was founded in 1921 for the employees of Shell: originally established at Teddington, it moved in 1923 and now occupies a neighbouring site, with its 1954 boathouse downstream; upstream, after Ranelagh Sailing Club, is the neat boathouse of **Vesta** RC, whose first premises, in 1870, at the mouth of the Wandle, about half a mile below Putney Bridge, were in an area well known for athletics and boating. However, industry and commerce made inroads, so the club moved to Ranelagh's building till 1890, when the present clubhouse was occupied.

Two members at that time became famous in different spheres: Harry Blackstaffe as a sculler, R.M. Hutchinson as the music hall's 'Harry Tate'. Rowing successes in the 1920 Wyfolds Final and 1930 Thames Cup at Henley, as well as many senior victories, were blunted only by a serious fire in 1936 which destroyed boats, furnishings and gear.

The boathouse's role during World War II was as a fire station, aptly, and later building landing-craft. Post-war successes included the juniors rising to seniors within a month in 1956, another Wyfolds Final, 1961, West of England Fours Challenge Cup, National Championships and Olympics representation in coxless fours. The club played its part too in promoting Tideway Events: the Vesta Dashes and the Scullers' Head being perhaps the most memorable.

Next to Vesta is the boathouse of **Thames** RC, which began in 1860 as the City of London RC. Originally using Simmons boathouse at Putney, in 1879 the club built the present premises, though the balcony has since been enclosed, with an eights rowing tank and gymnasium coming later. Thames first appeared at Henley in 1870, winning the Wyfold; successes have followed in profusion both in Britain and internationally. Until the 1920s amateur boxing was promoted in the Big Room, many professional champions gave exhibitions, and indeed a member, George Vize, became amateur heavyweight champion in 1878 after retiring from rowing and was subsequently President of the ABA. But then Thames has been fortunate in so many of its members; Jack Beresford Junior and Steve Fairbairn spring to mind. In other ways too the club has contributed to sport: a founder member of the Metropolitan Rowing Association, later the ARA, the club also founded the Thames Hare and Hounds in 1867 to encourage cross-country running as winter training. This club developed by 1880 into the Amateur Athletics Association.

No wonder Thames has won more than one Victor Ludorum. That they were in favour of women's events at the National Championships seems typical of the breadth of their influence.

With **Imperial College**'s this array of boathouses ends, Beverley Brook intervening before **Barn Elms Rowing Centre**, which

*Hammersmith's waterside has much history to go with its rowing activity. In the right-hand drawing the view from Sir Joseph Bazalgette's exuberant bridge shows the headquarters of the Amateur Rowing Association, and beside that Regency façade the bow window of 'the Priory', which London Transport RC uses. Along much of this stretch of the Thames precaution against flooding has meant having removable gates to the pontoons.*

*The left-hand illustration is of the Sons of the Thames' boathouse in Upper Mall, Hammersmith, with Kelmscott House on the farther side. Here lived William Morris the founder of the Arts & Crafts movement, and before him George MacDonald, whose fairy stories have delighted many children. Between these two buildings the little coach-house also has a place in history, for here the first electric telegraph was constructed in 1816 by Sir Francis Ronalds.*

caters for Inner London Education Authority schools crews.

HAMMERSMITH BRIDGE beyond Crab Tree Reach marks the beginning of the curve in the river that presents the major challenge during the University Boat Race. Indeed, the Old Bridge was a well-known viewing position, offering splendid opportunity to assess the crews' tactics. Just upstream is the second cluster of clubs. On the north bank **London Transport (CRS, Thames)** RC comes first, occupying a boathouse that is perhaps the most charming on the Tideway. Its bow window suggests the eighteenth century, though the club is much younger, dating from 1930, and next to it the headquarters of the **ARA**, with the same address of 6 Lower Mall, without the intriguing addition of 'The Priory'. The governing body of this country's rowing has occupied the premises since 1974, when the National Westminster Bank made it over. Here takes place some of the National Rowing Squad training, and from its elegant balcony many a Boat Race and Head have been expertly scrutinized.

Further along Lower Mall, next to the Blue Anchor, the **Auriol Kensington** RC boathouse consists of two riverside cottages over a century old, whose first-floor windows present a magnificent view stretching from Harrod's repository to Chiswick Eyot. The club too is a conversion, or amalgamation, for in 1981 Kensington RC, formed 1872, joined with Auriol, 1896. The component clubs in their early years used local inns for clubrooms, while the rowing was by hiring boats from local professionals. One such was Biffen, who owned the boathouse at 14 Lower Mall and lent accommodation to both clubs. When he died, in 1947, Auriol bought the entire premises.

Kensington, the senior club, had its own regatta from 1878 and indeed treasured its successes for it boasted a picture gallery of every winning crew from 1900 onwards. W.D. Kinnear was perhaps its most distinguished member, winner of the Olympic sculls in 1912.

Auriol too has its memories: some happy, as its trip to Boston, USA, as the first British crew to compete in the Head of the Charles River race in 1979; some sad, when a novice oar of 1948 and junior eights winner at the 1950 Hammersmith Regatta lost his life in a plane crash in 1975. He was a fine racer in another sport too, winning the motor-racing World Championship twice. His name? Graham Hill.

But the name most closely associated with rowing from Hammersmith must surely be Furnivall. Indeed, the gardens dividing Lower from Upper Mall are a perpetual reminder of Frederick J. Furnivall. A barrister, a social thinker who knew Ruskin, and a philologist, he made his contribution to the sport largely through an enthusiasm for sculling; with almost missionary zeal his converts were, willing or unwilling, made to see that being on the water was everything. He improved the design of the boat; he founded the NARA in 1891 and Hammersmith Sculling Club four years later. The present boathouse in Lower Mall bears his name in **Furnivall** SC, begun in 1896 as the Hammersmith Sculling Club for Girls and Men. Appropriately it shares its premises with the **Tideway Scullers School**, which dates from 1958. Before a National Squad was introduced, Tideway Scullers provided many of the international representatives. In some ways it has been

*Two boathouses in Lower Mall: Furnivall Sculling Club is by Furnivall Gardens, thus doubly ensuring that the name of the man who brought to sculling a missionary enthusiasm and who founded the NARA is never forgotten. Here too the Tideway Scullers School has its base; the other is of Auriol Kensington sandwiched between the Rutland and Blue Anchor, for this is a riverside well endowed with pubs.*

*Perhaps the most famous pub on Hammersmith's waterside is the Dove, seen on the right centre in this drawing. Not only did Sir A.P. Herbert, that boat-loving writer and Member of Parliament, frequent it, but it is for ever associated with the Doves Press, a pioneer in the revival of good printing. This scene includes Chiswick Eyot and Chiswick church, both landmarks in the University Boat Race and in the annual Tideway Head of the River which is rowed in the downstream direction.*

nomadic, relying on the hospitality of other clubs. Nevertheless, it is the only club to hold an annual sculling handicap race on the Thames; its members have won the Wingfield five times, and as eights – for it has a variety of rowing – the Head of the River, many Henley trophies and international events. But it is on sculling that the emphasis is placed, so the school is proposing a ten-year programme of expansion in this aspect. Furnivall would have approved.

The remaining clubs in Upper Mall are **Sons of the Thames** RC, founded in 1886, and **Latymer Upper School** BC, dating from 1937. On the Surrey side opposite, **St Paul's School**, 1881, and its Old Boys, **Colet** BC, provide this part of the reach with younger crews.

Beyond Chiswick Eyot, Corney Reach leads to Duke's Meadows, the start of the third group. By Barnes Railway Bridge stand the

121

*As everybody knows, the University Boat Race is from Putney to Mortlake. This first drawing shows the finish, with the Ship Tavern and the Stag Brewery prominent on the Surrey side. After the race the crews are hosted at the boathouses of Ibis and Quintin, pictured here from Chiswick Bridge. The tall tower in the distance is that of Kew Bridge pumping station.*

following clubs' boathouses: **Civil Service** LRC, founded 1927, together with **Cygnet** RC, 1890, **Emanuel School** BC, 1915, with its Old Boys **Dacre** BC, and **Chiswick School** BC, 1931, sharing with **Ealing High Schools** BC, 1946.

At Chiswick Bridge, on the Middlesex bank, **Ibis** RC and **Quintin** BC occupy neighbouring sites. The latter, formed in 1907, has an association with the Polytechnic of Central London, taking its name doubtless from the man so closely involved with that institution and the NARA, Quintin Hogg. The former is associated with Prudential Assurance; indeed, from its foundation in 1871 until 1984 membership was confined to employees. Legend has it that the name was the choice of a director of the company who had shot an ibis in North Africa. Mention of the club by Dickens referred to the time when it was located together with many other clubs, including Leander, at Biffen's Hammersmith boathouse. In 1886 the move to the present site, and the building of the boathouse in 1915, brought it moderate success only, partly because of the limited membership. The interruption of World War II, when the boathouse was requisitioned as an Army officers' mess and later by the Norwegian Mercantile Marine, was followed by many valiant attempts at Henley and the Tideway Head. As important as race wins may appear, the winning of rowing friends is also valuable; here Ibis has achieved much. The club has combined with Anglian for a senior pair win at the Metropolitan in 1952, with Mortlake for a similar success at Kingston in 1960, and every year two private matches are rowed with Mortlake-Anglian and Quintin.

And of course it must not be forgotten that, together with Quintin, Ibis hosts the University oarsmen after each Boat Race.

Further upstream in Kew Meadows are **Mortlake Anglian and Alpha** BC, and **Thames Tradesmen**'s RC, 1896, following the impressive headquarters of **London University** BC, with **London Hospital** RC on the north bank.

TUCKED UNDER THE LEE of Kew Bridge on the north bank is one of the most historic and well-equipped clubs, the **Horseferry** RC, for employees of the North Thames Gas Region.

In 1825 the land was leased to the nearby Star and Garter Inn, but by the turn of the century the site housed the Oxford and Cambridge public house and, more importantly, the Brentford Conservative RC boathouse, which is now Horseferry's. A long hut adjacent to the bridge had been built for the rowing members of Brentford gasworks; eventually, however, in 1920 the gas company acquired the site, and five years later it took over the present boathouse for its rowing section of the Athletic Association.

Like so many other clubs, the Gas Light and Coke Company's Sports Association Rowing Club, as it was styled in 1926, had its problems of affiliation, being first a member of Furnivall's NARA, though even then a number of oarsmen were deemed ineligible because they were professional.

In 1928 the Sports Association held its own regatta on home waters, the company providing new boats and landing stage. Successes followed at Hampton Regatta the same year, and in the following decade there were wins in NARA and Thames ARA regattas; at the Championship Regatta on the Henley course its senior eight won the Desborough Challenge Cup.

123

*The tall tower of Kew Bridge pumping station that can be seen from Chiswick Bridge is closely associated visually with Horseferry RC boathouse, as this drawing shows. A historical association is with the building on the extreme right of the page for this is the Star and Garter whose landlord back in 1825 leased the land on which the boathouse stands. Today it is the headquarters of North Thames Gas rowing, and the pumping station is a 'steam museum': so here is plenty of energy. The Horseferry Regatta itself has what might be termed an alternating current, for it is rowed from either side of Kew Bridge depending on the tide.*

When affiliation to the ARA became possible in 1938, it was necessary to change the club's name, 'Horseferry' being chosen because the company's chief office had been in Horseferry Road, Westminster.

After World War II the club resumed its regatta, and in 1984 a ladies' race was introduced, resulting in a dead heat. Joining with Ibis, Cygnet and London Transport Clubs, in 1971 Horseferry launched the first of the many Business Houses Regattas.

The club has had many colourful personalities: one, a captain and founder member, sculled till his eighties, when he capsized and, being a non-swimmer, decided to 'call it a day'! But perhaps the strangest incident to involve a member took place in 1942, in mid Atlantic. An occupant of an open boat among the survivors from the torpedoed merchant ship *Muncaster Castle* discovered he had rowed, as bow in a junior eight of Gas Light, in the 1935 Weybridge Regatta, against another survivor, also bow!

DATING FROM 1860, **Twickenham** RC has as its address Eel Pie Island. Perhaps few other clubs have so intriguing a mix of the homely and the highborn, for the land was originally owned by the exiled King of France, who then lived in Orleans House, as the Duc d'Aumale. He gave the freehold to the club, which in gratitude

*Teddington Lock marks the upper limit of the tidal Thames, and so Twickenham represents the end of Tideway rowing. The home of rowing here is Eel Pie Island, its name derived apparently from the practice of selling those delicacies to day-trippers from London who came up on the pleasure steamers in Victorian times. Although the inn which dispensed them has gone, and smart townhouses face the mainstream, the side of the island pictured here still has its boatyard and the rowing club. It fortunately preserves an atmosphere itself as well as looking across to the 1714 church and York House rebuilt in 1700, having been the residence of a Lord Chancellor, the Earl of Clarendon. In the drawing the tower beyond the footbridge is of St Catherine's convent school where Alexander Pope's villa once stood.*

*Many artists have been inspired to paint the Thames from Richmond Hill. This view is at the riverside with that hill on the distant right. Glovers Island opposite Petersham Meadows provides a discernible group of trees, while on the left Marble Hill House is a dramatic punctuation point on this splendid stretch of water. The house was built in 1729 by Henrietta Howard, mistress of George II, its gardens landscaped by Bridgeman. Nearby is the site of the original Orleans House where such nobility as Louis-Philippe, the Duc de Montpensier, the Comte de Beaujolais and Don Carlos spent some time. Today these grounds are enjoyed by the public, and particularly on the occasions of the Twickenham and Richmond regattas. Few stretches claim to be such a 'course of history'.*

made him its first president.

In 1923 a regatta was established including in its title Richmond. However, in 1950 a division occurred when Richmond decided to hold its own regatta. The Twickenham course is two thirds of a mile (1,100 metres), starting just below Glovers Island and finishing at Orleans Gardens, where the enclosure is set. As the river is semi-tidal here, there is normally a tide change at some time in the day's racing. The Richmond course is in reverse direction, beginning at Orleans Gardens and continuing to Buccleuch Gardens beside the Three Pigeons public house.

Both courses use one of the most beautiful parts of the Thames, with Marble Hill Park on the Middlesex bank and the grounds of Ham House on the Surrey side. This stretch must indeed be known to thousands of people through the much-photographed view from the top of Richmond Hill.

Incidentally, Twickenham RC has helped to preserve another feature of the Thames scene by its hospitality to the Skiff Club, whose members use the wide, fixed-seat craft that are so important a facet of the local river life.

# CHAPTER TEN

## *Lower Thames and South-East*

POPLAR · GREENWICH · GRAVESEND · ROCHESTER
· CHATHAM · DOVER · FOLKESTONE

ENCOURAGED BY THE PROFUSION of oared craft on Greenwich
Reach and the possibility of employment on the docks, in 1854 a
group of young men formed **Poplar, Blackwall and District** RC.
Their fathers obtained some old two- and four-oar gigs, and the
rowing began. Initially the club's base was in the Lifeboat public
house, but during the following eighty years many other, similar
premises served, until eventually Calders Wharf in Cubitt Town,
opposite the Royal Naval College and Curlew RC, became home.
From the old railway shed which was originally secured, progress,
through the LCC and the Sports Council, resulted in a £70,000
boathouse of the 1970s. Its rowing, training and social facilities are
exceptional, the envy of most clubs elsewhere, and the pride of the
Isle of Dogs.

At one time it was primarily a dockers' club under the National
Dock Labour Board and Tradesmen's Rowing Association, but
now it is open to all. Amongst its many successes must be recorded
Doggett's Coat and Badge wins, that oldest annual rowing contest
indeed, oldest annual sporting event in Britain, as indeed might be
expected with a club that maintains a high standard of competitive
rowing on the Lower Thames.

WHEN CANON MILLER became the incumbent of Greenwich, it
was not long before he decided to form a rowing club. A

*Curlew RC has today a base that basks in the glory of its near neighbour, the Royal Naval College at Greenwich. Here the splendid river frontage of Sir Christopher Wren's hospital for old seamen is complemented by the Trafalgar Tavern of 1837, whose façade of verandas and canopies is echoed by Curlew's raft. The whole setting is saturated with things nautical, for at the western end of the river walk, beyond Wren's building, the famous Clipper Ship 'Cutty Sark' and Chichester's 'Gypsy Moth' yacht that circumnavigated the world have found their haven.*

Cambridge oarsman himself, his enthusiasm resulted in **Curlew RC**.

The year of its foundation was 1866, a date shared by a number of other clubs, but it did not mark the beginning of rowing here, for there had been local watermen's regattas at Greenwich for at least a century, and several small one-boat clubs, such as Lurlines and Argonaut, both of which joined with Curlew. The name was taken from its first boat's, itself a reminder of the bird frequenting the marshy area.

At first the club used the Crown and Sceptre public house as its headquarters, an old Port of London Authority barge serving to

128

store the boats, but after World War II it found a home at the Trafalgar Hotel, near the Royal Naval College, and today it has a purpose-built clubhouse a few yards from the Trafalgar Tavern. A hut some fifty yards down the river has the boats, while the old raft is still there off the spit of shingle. How long this will remain is uncertain, for the lease-owners, Watneys, have plans to build a wine bar on the club site.

LIKE CANON MILLER, when Mr Simes moved from Hastings to Greenwich to set up a corn and seed merchant's business, he determined to continue as an oarsman. So in the summer of 1878 **Gravesend** RC was formed. Influential citizens were attracted, new boats ordered and in a short while the first race was underway between *Mermaid, Sunbeam* and *Neptune*. How it ended is not clear because someone fired a gun before the three miles had been covered and the leader stopped rowing. At the town regatta that same year Curlew RC from Greenwich constituted the first opponents, and not surprisingly overwhelmed the fledgelings.

Defeat did nothing to reduce enthusiasm, particularly as the club's patron was the Honourable Ivo Bligh, afterwards Earl of Darnley, who had taken the first England cricket team to Australia in 1861 and lost.

*The lower reaches of the Thames have their homes of rowing, and Gravesend must be one of the most historic, for the clubhouse was on land belonging to the War Office, being part of the New Tavern Fort which General Gordon had rebuilt in 1871. Permission for the club to go ahead was given by the commanding officer, himself a member, though there was the stipulation that the structure should not exceed eleven feet in height in order that the coastal defence guns in the fort might have a clear field of fire over the top. Consequently the squat wood and corrugated iron building caused some adverse comments, and it was not until 1912 that the present lantern roof was added.*

*Today the scene has changed, with the new tower of the Port of London Authority Thames Navigation Service beyond the causeway and the old Sea School site, while to the left of the clubhouse in this drawing the eighteenth-century customs and excise house can be seen neighbouring the mound that marks the fort.*

Accommodation for the new club members was found temporarily at the Commercial Hotel, conveniently close to the river, it being recorded that soap and towels were provided for 18 shillings a week. However, the club prospered enough for proposals to be made that it should have its own boatshed, and later clubhouse, on the foreshore nearby.

One interesting feature of those early years was the change, in the mid-80s, from river to coastal racing, and after a few years back again, a change possibly unique in rowing history and not unconnected with the problems of transporting boats in those days, as well as taking Mr Simes' Hastings experience into account. Incidentally the club has recently competed in occasional coastal regattas in borrowed boats, for being situated as it is on the Lower Thames, the nearest club to the sea and receiving its full share of rough water, there is something to be said for a change back yet again to coastal rowing. In fact, in the early years two members were drowned when a pair capsized, so to encourage swimming ability a silver cup, the Cooper, was presented for an annual swimming race. It is still competed for, with a similar trophy for women.

As might be expected in this area, professional rowing was considerable; an example of the survival can be seen in the fact that in 1984 the club secretary, Eric Lupton, was a Doggett's Coat and Badge winner of 1941; when he beat Eric Phelps in 1954, he became the last holder of the European title. Further, both his sons, Harold Smith and Jack Anson all won the Coat and Badge and are members.

The future of the club seems assured, but that of the boathouse, historic as it is, cannot be. From here crews have gone to Henley and the National Championships.

For many years the club's regatta course started at the old 'explosives noticeboard' just below the famous Ship and Lobster public house, Denton, finishing nine furlongs along at the clubhouse. This extremely long stretch was reduced to half a mile

*Rochester's rowing has its headquarters at a location of great significance to aeronautical historians, for it uses the slipway where once the flying boats of the famous firm of Short Brothers were launched. In this illustration the twin landmarks of Rochester's castle and cathedral, both dating from Norman times, can be seen to the right of the bridge.*

when the jetty was built in 1965, occasioning a renaming to Sprint Regatta. Perhaps this change of title was useful as it distinguished the club's regatta from the town regatta, when traditional four-oared watermen's skiffs are used. Six of these 21-foot heavy clinker-built boats are still owned by the regatta committee. Included in the events during the year is the Long Ferry Race from Westminster to Gravesend, retracing the route granted exclusively to Gravesend watermen by royal charter in 1401. The Gravesend RC may not be as old as the town regatta, which can claim records back to 1698, but it enjoys a water every bit as historic.

MOST ROWING CLUBS have had 'lean' years, but few can have been in such a precarious situation as the Medway RC found itself in during 1883: one four and a sinking raft. This club, formed in 1865, had since the earliest years rowed from near Rochester Bridge; by 1864 it was particularly successful with trial races and open regattas and doubtless by its example encouraged the formation of another club downstream. This, the Chatham Mechanics Institute RC, also did well − perhaps having the son of Charles Dickens as President helped. In 1872 it felt 'amateur' enough to break with its parent institute, call itself Chatham RC and admit to membership gentlemen. However, by 1877 there was amalgamation with another club, Gillingham, because both were losing support. A fair resolution of identity came with Chatham keeping its name and Gillingham its colours.

Both Medway and Chatham Club rafts had problems, not only from storms but also vandalism and corrosion. In 1887 Medway secured a new one, but amazingly Chatham's survived two World Wars before finally bowing to age, while Medway's lasted till the 1950s. Strangely it was the rafts that eventually led to the amalgamation of these two clubs, after much agonizing and temporary alliance, so a hut was bought from the Royal Engineers and erected on its present site at the slipway where the great Empire Class flying-boats of Short Brothers were launched. Incidentally, the **Royal Engineers** RC, which dates from 1846, competed on this stretch of the Medway until 1961.

So in 1965 **Medway Towns** RC celebrated its centenary, and since then it has enjoyed successes, bought new boats, refurbished its

*Dover holds its regatta against a background as dramatic and historic as anywhere in the country. High above the outer harbour the castle, 'England's Key', with its Church of St Mary de Castro and the Roman pharos (lighthouse) at its west end, looks down on Waterloo Crescent and Marine Parade where the rowing club has its boathouse on the beach.*

boathouse and attracted the attention of scullers from a wide area. After all, one member, Captain Frank Bebbington, had attempted to scull across the English Channel in 1907 – and he managed to cover half the distance before wind and waves undid him!

Regatta courses have varied: Chatham used its reach and later, when its amalgamation with Gillingham took place, moved to Sovereign Reach downstream. Medway's first regatta course was from the Mile Tree near the present boathouse to the Esplanade, and later from Cuxton upstream to the site of Medway Fort. Today the row starts on the rising tide from Rochester Pier to the boathouse, crews having to negotiate the S-shaped bends without cutting the corner on the north shore and being caught in slack water off Temple Marsh.

The Head of the River race, which used to take place from Upnor to the raft at the end of the Esplanade, has moved to a course between Maidstone Church and Allington Lock – a pity, for this water has a long history and a setting ideal for rowing.

THERE IS SOMETHING intriguing about seniority, and the claims of one organization to be the oldest. However, in the matter of the oldest coastal rowing club there can be no controversy: **Dover** RC formed in 1846, long before the harbour was built, and indeed

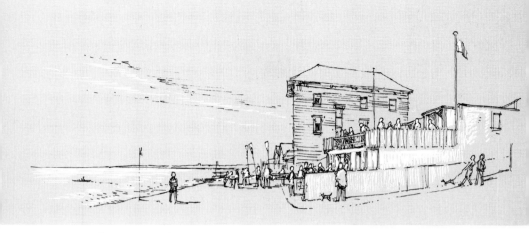

*Folkestone RC has its premises at Sandgate, a mile or so to the west of the town. Here coastline and sky almost merge as the vista swings round to Hythe and Romney Marsh.*

before all but four inland rowing clubs were in existence.

Strange, then, that so little is known of the early years, as it was not till the 1880s that the club's activities were chronicled. Perhaps the earliest fact concerns not success in a regatta but, as befits the locality, a cross-Channel row: when, in 1885, an Oxford University crew made the first crossing in an eight, the cox to steer them safely over was from Dover RC.

For the record, Dover won the senior fours 1892-5 and 1907-11, but it was not until the last decade or so that success has become more frequent. Perhaps now that it has a new boathouse, opened in 1983 at the western end of the harbour, a new era will open too, for it is an historic place.

Also historic is the water of the regatta: it is one and a half miles (about 2,300 metres) with a turn, starting and finishing opposite the Royal Cinque Ports Yacht Club. There are turning buoys at the eastern end of the harbour. This racing turn is a distinctive feature, making for spectacular scenes when it is remembered that up to twelve crews can race abreast.

FOLKESTONE SEEMS RELUCTANT to accommodate its sportsmen: the

134

racecourse is at Westenhanger, the cricket ground at Cheriton and **Folkestone** RC at Sandgate. Of course there could well be a reason, for so far as rowing is concerned the cliffs have given way to easier access, and the boathouse stands but twenty yards from the beach – with the attendant risk of flooding in winter.

Formed in 1852, that club has always been strong at senior level, winning the *Daily Herald* cup five times, though at junior it did not do badly, to win in 1955 the Junior Four Championship of Great Britain.

Interestingly, the club's senior four of 1966 rowed in the only dead heat for the Bideford Bowl at Bournemouth.

CHAPTER ELEVEN

## Hampshire, Isle of Wight and Dorset

### SOUTHSEA · RYDE · SOUTHAMPTON
### CHRISTCHURCH · BLANDFORD

SOMETIME BEFORE 1860 a Dr Fowler gathered together a group of gentlemen to practise rowing in four-oared boats from Clarence Beach, Southsea. When in 1860 four of them decided to organize their activity, the **Southsea** RC was formed; a small hut was rented from the War Department, which then owned all the sea front, and so began the occupation of site that has lasted ever since. In 1872 a proper boathouse was built out of dockyard timber, to house the fours, pairs and skiffs. Coastal rowing was now expanding: witness the annual race against Portsmouth RC over a five-mile course in the Solent, and the South Coast Championship, for singles and doubles.

By the 1880s the club was one of the most influential in the area, with the Duke of Connaught and Earl of Clanwilliam its patrons, three baronets, an MP and five JPs among its members. Rules regarding dress were strict, as were times for Sunday bathing and boating, so as not to offend the promenaders.

A cup still exists showing that the Portsmouth and Southsea Regatta was being held in 1839, with events for amateurs and professional wherrymen and fishermen, as well as naval cutters. These regattas attracted enormous crowds; special excursion trains were put on, boats being transported on timber wagons free of charge. However, when this concession was withdrawn, the sliding-seat four that had been acquired from Clasper's in the 1880s

136

was impracticable. So fixed-seat rowing predominated in the Solent until 1925, when a new sliding-seat coastal four was ordered. But the older boats were not easily superseded: a 1904 coastal stagger seat clasper survived exposure, sinking, ramming by an umpire's boat, even an incendiary bomb, until 1958. Its bow has been preserved.

The old wooden boathouse was not so fortunate, suffering at the time of the Mulberry Harbour construction in the last war, and in 1959, just as the club was preparing for its centenary celebrations, it was burned, together with the boats, equipment and records. In the face of this deliberate destruction, resolution and help came from all members. Plans had already been prepared for a new building, and by accelerating the process the official opening took place in centenary year. Many local clubs lent boats and blades; George Feltham, over eighty years old, built two new thirty-foot clinker

*Rowers at Southsea have no rafts to launch from but wade straight into the water, chest high if it is rough. Their regatta takes place at South Parade pier, but the boathouse is further to the west, where at Clarence Beach its companions are not only 'Victory's' Anchor and the hovercraft terminal but also the vast amusement park by the Clarence Pier.*

*Ryde RC on the Isle of Wight has made its headquarters in Appley Park, to the east of the resort's centre. Here the two drawings show, on the left, the stone boathouse that is rented from the borough. It was originally part of the Appley Estate and at one time housed the four-oar galleys belonging to a private school, the Isle of Wight College; hence the illustration's lighter approach. The other drawing of the clubhouse also in Appley Park has a more conventional appearance, though its location a hundred yards from the sea cannot make for much levity. Ryde's third building is nearer the sea but further from Ryde, being at Cowes.*

fixed seats, probably the last to be made in Britain, a whole spruce tree being shipped over from Vancouver.

Many well-known people have been associated with the club: Sir Alec Rose, who returned from his round-the-world voyage to a special jetty alongside the club, Captain John Ridgeway and Chay Blyth, also made life members after their transatlantic row, and Graham Hill, the motor-racing driver, who counted this club his second home from Auriol Kensington.

Since the end of World War II, the regatta has moved to the eastern end of Southsea's five-mile sea front, as shipping congestion increases, but it too grows, with 300 crews taking part. Dr Fowler would have been proud of what he started over 125 years ago.

AN OAR CAN BE SEEN in the bar of Yelf's Hotel, Union Street, Ryde, on the Isle of Wight, for it was here in 1877 that twenty-five gentlemen decided to form a **Ryde** RC. The next year a boatman was hired for 16 shillings a week and a boathouse leased at the end the pier. In 1905 another site, shared with the lifeboat, Vectis BC, coastguards and Missions to Seamen, was inaugurated. Expansion took over some of these other premises, resulting in a reading-room, ladies' dressing-room and further additions. It also served as a first-aid post during the Schneider Trophy races. However, in 1968 British Railways, the latest landlord, decided the boathouse was unsafe, so in 1970 a small stone boathouse in Appley Park was rented. Nevertheless, the club was determined to have its own building and, thanks to support from many inside and outside the membership, a new headquarters was opened in 1975, though the Appley Park premises were retained and moreover another was acquired at Cowes.

The rowing at Ryde takes various forms: there is the competitive, against other clubs, at Henley — where in 1858 the Ryde sculler Sweatman experienced his sliding seat disintegrate — and of course at the South Coast Championships. Another activity is rowing around the island, some fifty-eight miles. In 1932 this was achieved by a crew of five in eight hours forty minutes; in 1965 it was thirty-four minutes faster!

THE ITCHEN RIVER at Southampton has been associated with shipping for centuries, so it is not surprising that a number of rowing clubs have grown up here. One, the **British Transport Commission (Southampton)** RC, founded in 1927, has its boathouse actually in one of the berths at East Docks; another is closely connected with a shipbuilding firm, while the remaining two have sites beside the bridges that span the river.

**Southampton** ARC was begun in 1945 and has its boathouse on the Woolston bank by the Itchen Bridge, looking across to the newly rebuilt boathouse of **Vosper Thornycroft** ARC. It holds its regatta on a course which goes under the bridge.

But the club which has the longest history is the 'Coalies' — the **Southampton Coalporters** ARC. Over 110 years ago the first members were the coalporters who rowed barges of coal to the great steamships that docked in this port, and clearly their preoccupation with the activity did not end with work, for by 1865 they had established an annual regatta, off Chapel. Then, when in 1884 the United States frigate *Lancaster* was lying in Southampton Water, a challenge race was fixed between its champion crew and the club. For stakes of £60, the five-mile course was agreed: from the Royal Pier to Netley Hospital and back; and the crews were decided, namely fourteen American, eighteen coalporters, together with coxes. The apparent disparity was more than compensated for by the fact that the Americans were an unbeaten team trained for just this kind of contest, having a specially designed racing boat, whereas the coalporters had to borrow a disused service cutter from the condemned stores at Portsmouth dockyard! Amid fever pitch

*It is to be expected that Southampton's plenitude of water has resulted in rowing. These drawings evidence two clubs that enjoy the River Itchen. On the left, Southampton Coalporters boathouse by Northam Bridge may claim to be nearest the original site of the city, Clausentum, and its own beginning is a fascinating story of courage, determination and pride. The other drawing shows the view from Southampton ARC premises, looking across the river to St Mary's, the mother church of the port and, incidentally, the 'Saints' football club.*

140

*Christchurch, like Southampton, is at the confluence of two rivers, in this case the Avon and Stour. Here the emphasis is very much on pleasure boating with all the problems of crowding it brings. However, the rowing club has a fine headquarters, and it is not likely to abandon its location at Wick Lane, near the magnificent priory church.*

excitement, with spectators crowding quays, piers and craft, the 'Coalies' won. When a return match for even higher stakes had the same result, it was not long before the Portsmouth Shovellers challenged them to yet another five-mile race.

Such contests gave place inevitably to the more conventional river and coastal rowing, where coalporters have acquitted themselves throughout the years: for example winning the Desborough Cup and being runners up in the *Daily Herald* competition. Where the club was less fortunate was in its boathouse. For years it had been an old wooden ammunition barge with a corrugated iron superstructure. On one occasion in 1953 it broke loose, ran aground and was saved from breaking up on the ebb tide only by the umpire's launch towing it to safety. Then in the 1960s the new land-based boathouse was built, by Northam Bridge, and the regatta course start established nearby.

Today 'Coalies' continue the great tradition of last century and deserve that description of 1884: 'The Coal Porters, who won in spite of difficulties which seemed to so heavily handicap them, gave evidence of undeveloped powers as oarsmen for which their most prejudiced admirers would scarcely have given them credit.' How appropriate that the first boat was called *Black Diamond*, a symbol still to be seen on the club's blades.

WHEN, SHORTLY after **Christchurch** RC was formed in 1948, a gift was made to it of a small piece of waterlogged land off Willow Way, it seemed hardly worth accepting. Members thought its value about a £1. Yet many years later its sale brought thousands of pounds to the club and led the way to the building of a fine, fully equipped clubhouse at Wick Ferry in 1965. Certainly Christchurch deserved their luck, for a Nissen-type hut had served as a temporay store, and indeed in the first year there were not boats anyway. Thanks to the offer of Bournemouth's Westover RC, the new club enjoyed honorary membership, thus becoming eligible to use boats and accommodation there. However, it was not long before Christchurch had acquired its own boats, albeit fixed seat, and begun competing.

Today the river seems so crowded with pleasure craft, even during the regatta, that the thought of moving elsewhere must suggest itself to the members. But such are their enthusiasm and the memory of those early years that Wick Ferry is going to see many more years of rowing. After all, in a novice four race back in 1948, the Christchurch stroke was heard to say, 'A yacht came in close. I hit it with my oar and fell off my sliding seat!'

JUST ON THE SOUTHERN edge of Blandford stands the impressive gateway built by James Wyatt in 1775 for the Portman family. The road through it leads, eventually, to the great mansion, now a school. This is Bryanston, and its neo-Wren sumptuousness, to the design of Norman Shaw in the 1890s, looks over sweeping grass to the River Stour. From its foundation in January 1928 there has been a **Bryanston School** BC, thanks to the first headmaster who brought with him from Westminster School Ronnie King, who built up the club gradually, delaying entry to outside competition till he was satisfied with the standard. Such discretion had its reward in 1948 when, at Henley in the Ladies' Plate, Bryanston and Eton contested the final, probably the only time this century it has been between two schools. That year also saw an Old Boy row in the Olympics coxed pairs; it is said that Bodley-Scott and his partner sawed off the rudder, to prevent the cox disturbing the run of the boat. Other Olympic oars and one University dark and light Blue – he rowed for both – are examples of the fine tradition of the

142

*Bryanston School's rowing has a beautiful setting by the River Stour. Blandford town seems miles away, though the busy road to Shaftesbury makes its presence known across the water. On the school side all is peaceful pasture and parkland, the rustic character of the boatshed in the foreground contributing to the rural charm.*

club here.

As to the boathouse, its situation is delightful. The River Stour, so it is said, was moved by Viscount Portman some hundred yards because he feared his house would be damp. Probably the truth is that the landscaping including digging out and deepening the mill stream, for this a slow-moving chalk river. Anyway, the result is a stretch of water wider, straighter and deeper than any other part of the river. Nevertheless, it is still one of the smallest waters used by a rowing school, being about two miles (3,220 metres), with a straight of only a third of a mile (500 metres). At first the boats were simply kept under the trees, then an old army hut was acquired, set on three-foot tree stumps to keep it above flood level, and in 1949 a boy-built boathouse opened. Twelve years later 'industrial type' building was added.

Ronnie King's 'reign' ended in 1953, and Bill Phelps', as boatman, in 1952. But the club goes on, its successes extending beyond Henley – where it shared a record time to Fawley in the Schools Special Race – to Connecticut, Kent School, USA.

*Coate Water Park at Swindon may be the venue for Bradford-on-Avon's regatta but its rowing home is still very much the delightful setting of the stone-built town. As this drawing shows, the view from the boathouse at Barton Farm includes not only a picturesque bridge but also the splendid tithe barn.*

144

# CHAPTER TWELVE

## *West*

### BRADFORD-ON-AVON · BRISTOL · GLOUCESTER TEWKESBURY

ALTHOUGH WHEN AVON RC at Trowbridge was founded, in 1865, it was reported there were young men proficient in rowing at Bradford-on-Avon, they had a few more years to wait before their racing on the river above Avoncliff Weir was organized, by the formation of a **Bradford-on-Avon** RC in 1873. The club prospered, and its regatta soon collected the impressive set of fine silver cups still competed for today.

Like most clubs it suffered setbacks in interest and membership; here it seems the bowling section kept it going. Also, not uncommon, its boathouse was destroyed by fire, in 1962. This has been replaced, of course, although the clubhouse at St Margaret Street has simply been sold.

So Barton Bridge is now the rowing headquarters, and there are many clubs who would envy its situation. Nevertheless, Bradford is looking further afield: Coate Water Park near Swindon has been the venue for a regatta since 1981, interestingly resurrecting the name of a rowing club of earlier this century and of course reminding the visitor that it was here that Richard Jefferies, author of *Bevis*, lived.

BOATHOUSES AS THE BASES of rowing vary considerably in size, type and origin. In the case of **Bristol Ariel** RC, its first home, when it was founded in 1870, was a barge captured during the Napoleonic Wars and moored by Bristol Bridge. Such a location,

*St Anne's Park, Bristol, lies on the south-east side of the city, with the River Avon cutting a deep channel between wooded cliffs. Such a setting provides the Ariel rowing club with an idyllic location for its premises. These drawings show the old boathouse, the clubhouse as well as the pumping-station and sluice beyond. The smaller drawing, taken from above the river, is of the railway that momentarily emerges from its tunnels to share the scene.*

subject to the perils and odours of the floating harbour, left much to be desired, so it was not long before the club moved. A boathouse was built at St Anne's Park, in an area that preserved something of a rural setting. Today little has changed, although the expanding fleet of boats necessitated an addition to the building in 1970.

Ariel's home waters, the Hanham and Netham reach of the River Avon, run through deeply cut valleys, whose banks are densely wooded as far as Conham Bend where a sweeping arc in front of the boathouses takes the river into East Bristol's industrial area. About 1½ miles downstream from here the river divides and, by means of Netham Lock, maintains the supply of fresh water through the floating harbour.

Back in 1890 Ariel and what was then Avon RC, founded five years earlier than Ariel, organized a regatta on the River Avon at Saltford near Keynsham. With the passing years, pleasure traffic increased, as did the annual deficit, so that by the early 1970s this event was abandoned. But in 1975 Ariel, **Avon County** RC (1972), **City of Bristol** RC (1952) and **Bristol University** BC (1909) combined to organize a new Bristol Avon Regatta using a course in the city docks which had been closed previously. This change has worked, for the last decade has not revealed any loss in support. Perhaps that barge might have come in useful after all.

FOUNDED IN 1846, the **Gloucester RC** at first used the long reach on the Severn at Sandhurst north-west of the city. Today its

*The Gloucester and Berkeley Canal ends at Gloucester docks, having followed a course parallel to the Bristol road for the last few miles. In this drawing the rowing club's premises can be seen, with the cathedral tower in the distance. It would not be considered a beautiful stretch of water even by the most ardent Gloucester member, but it is not without character.*

*Cheltenham College rows at Tewkesbury, from a boathouse that stands well up on the bank. Nevertheless, it has not escaped the floods, as a mark on its walls records. Perhaps there was an appropriateness in its wartime use in fitting out RAF rescue launches here. The wooden structure looks across the river to the Lower Loade Hotel at Forthampton, where a ferry once operated. It is a spacious setting, enhanced by the distant presence of Tewkesbury Abbey as well as the nearer site of the momentous battlefield of the Wars of the Roses in 1471.*

boathouse stands on land owned by British Waterways at Hempstead beside the Gloucester and Sharpness Canal, sharing the location with King's School.

The two annual events are the Head of the River in February and regatta in August. For the former, the 2½-mile course starts at the Pilot Bridge, which the crews must pass, one at a time, the faster having precedence over a slower boat, and so through Rea and Sims bridges to the finish at the boathouse. Not only do tight bends cause problems for boats but there have been at least two years when ice has meant cancellation of the race.

For the regatta the problems arise mainly from pleasure craft seeking to share the water, but the course a straight two-thirds of a mile (thousand metres) more than compensates for this by its excellent regularity. After the finish there is a bridge to negotiate twice before landing.

THE FIRST ENTRY in the minute book of **Cheltenham College** BC

gives the circumstances of its foundation in 1859 as, 'Six gentlemen knowing the facilities for boating at Tewkesbury on the Avon and being fond of the pastime were accustomed to make up a crew and to test their mind and muscles by a twelve mile grind on the Avon or Severn in a boat.' According to the rules of the club, members wishing to row had to give to the captain not only their names but also the railway fare. This was important, for the college boathouse is not conveniently near; indeed, Lower Lode on the Severn (or is it Avon?) is some ten miles away. However, it was deemed sufficiently close to Tewkesbury to warrant a rider to the rules thus: 'It is particularly desirable that Public Houses in Tewkesbury should not be visited.' Since the membership was open to masters as well as boys, and in fact at least two were former Oxford University oarsmen, the directive presumably had some qualifications.

In those early years boats were stored at Bathurst's in Tewkesbury, yet despite this limitation the enthusiasm showed itself in the number of outside regattas and internal contests the college engaged in. In 1875 it took part in Tewkesbury Regatta, almost its first public appearance. Up till then there had been an annual race against Shrewsbury School at the town's regatta, or at home, though later Hereford, Worcester and Bridgnorth were additional venues to alleviate the travelling. Henley was attempted in 1877, but the opposition, Jesus College and Eton, proved too great, particularly for 'six' – champagne had to be supplied after he came round! Good came out of this and the following year's defeat: the

Henley authorities were persuaded to create a Public Schools Race, for fours admittedly rather than eights, but Cheltenham had the better of Radley and returned to a heroes' welcome with 'each member of the crew being carried on the steady shoulders of their school fellows across the playground'. This euphoria did not last, and the following years witnessed a decline in successes and support, particularly by the rowing masters. 'Bumps' were tried in 1884, the Shrewsbury race was re-introduced, and Henley faded, not least because the Public Schools Cup was now an event at Marlow Regatta.

Following success at Marlow four times in the inter-war period, and through the generosity of an old Cheltonian, the club was able to possess its own boathouse by the end of the 1920s. An interregnum by the RAF in World War II, when assembling of rescue launches had precedence over rowing, was succeeded by an era, one in which eights was restored and Henley, as well as the Tideway Head, once more appeared in the calendar. Moreover, a new club was born, the **Caterpillars**, which afforded opportunities for out-of-term rowing. But the best was yet to come, and those years of being 'also-runs' finally had an injection of success in 1984 when the National Schools Regatta saw Cheltenham win the Childe-Beal Cup; Henley saw a win in the semi-final with only a half-length defeat in the final – against Shrewsbury; and the coxless four represented England in the Countries International at Dublin, defeating Wales, Ireland and Scotland.

CHAPTER THIRTEEN

*Devon and Cornwall*

DARTMOUTH · BIDEFORD · FOWEY · FALMOUTH

ESTABLISHED IN 1869, **Dartmouth** ARC may confidently claim to be the oldest in the West of England. So far as identity is concerned, it has a history of independent existence second to none and has never been amalgamated with other clubs.

Its founder members built their own boat, winning their first cup the following year – a cup which, incidentally, is used to 'christen' each new boat. The cataloguing of success in the West of England and the South Coast Championships would be extensive proof of the achievements this senior club has attracted, but it would not be the whole story for Dartmouth played an important part in the formation of the West of England Amateur Rowing Association, in 1896 providing its first chairman and secretary.

Thirty-five years before the club came into existence, a meeting at the Castle Hotel in Dartmouth decided to hold a regatta in the harbour. Included in the events for rowers was a race for two-oared boats crewed by 'old men of 60 years and upwards'. Five entries were recorded.

In 1856 the royal yacht, with Queen Victoria, Prince Albert and other members of the royal family on board, anchored off the New Ground on the eve of the regatta. The opportunity was too good to miss, and that evening, when the royal party came ashore, the regatta committee presented the Queen with a programme 'tastefully printed on white satin'. Although the party left next day before the events started, two benefits resulted: a £25 gift for a race between sailors of Dartmouth, and the prefix 'Royal'. The only thing to mar that day was that the Mayor and his family returned home to find his silver and plate and the Corporation loving cup stolen.

Despite the predominance of sailing in the ensuing decades, rowing events continued to expand. There was, for example, the Grand Challenge Prize for four-oar gigs 'open to all the world'. Then, after World War I, the club had its heyday, highlighted in 1933 when, after a victorious regatta, both senior and junior crews competed at the London championships. They also combined to

*This view of Dartmouth is from the Higher ferry which links Kingswear to the town. The Royal Naval College cannot be seen from this position despite its elevated position and massive bulk, but the rowing club does feature. When the Royal Regatta takes place, this club and boathouse, despite its secluded corner, become a centre of activity and attention, even if there are so many other attractions.*

*On Monday 25 August 1834 a public breakfast was held in the Castle Hotel, Dartmouth, at which the 'respectable families of the neighbourhood', it was reported, decided to hold a sailing race for lighters and rowing races, including one for 'old men of 60 and upwards', which attracted five entries. Thus the annual regatta began, growing into the elaborate occasion of today.*

*Bideford's regatta may be older than Darmouth's, but its two rowing clubs are younger. The second drawing shows Bideford ARC headquarters, Manor Wharf. On the other side of the narrow Ropewalk there is the old custom house.*

enter the eights event and, without having trained together, won the Lord Desborough Cup for the All-England Championship. Two years later the seniors won the *Daily Herald* NARA cup for fours.

Though these regattas have gradually accrued a multitude of events ranging from motor-launch racing to water polo, athletics to tennis, central to them all have been sailing and rowing. Attitudes have changed, not only towards veteran oarsmen but also to women competitors. Back in 1856, when there was an event for women, the reporter's comment was that it proved 'amusing only from the costumes'.

THE RIVER TORRIDGE is wide as it flows down to the famous bridge

153

*No view of the River Torridge at Bideford can omit the famous fourteenth-century bridge, with its twenty-four arches all differing in their widths. This illustration, from the rowing club's converted warehouse premises, shows the 677-foot-long bridge, but it cannot also indicate the regatta course for new building to the left obscures the view. Perhaps one day an extension will be made allowing the members to regain their prospect from the Quay. However, even if that happens, another problem may arise when a new bridge materializes downstream.*

at Bideford. The town, though small, has two rowing clubs: they use the same stretch of water, differentiating themselves by their colours. The 'Blues' are the **Bideford** AAC, so there is the combination of activities to make demands on their clubhouse, while the 'Reds' maintain in their title a focus as **Bideford** ARC.

Each year a town regatta is held, records showing it was in existence by 1821. The other regatta is of much more recent date and was intended to be simply a celebration of the Reds' centenary in 1982, but it proved so popular that now it forms the second day of the town's. Perhaps the most memorable occasion came in 1955, when the last National Championship for the *Daily Herald* cup was raced here and the Reds won it. Generously the regatta committee provided a successor, the Bideford Bowl, which now ranks as the senior event in the South Coast Championship.

The early history of the Reds is obscure, a number of locations being recorded: Pollard's yard at East-the-Water, the Donkey yard, the Pill. Today the clubhouse is Manor Wharf, a building full of character – and hard work, for the members themselves did much of the restoration and alterations in 1976. But already there are plans to extend the front, for it is ironic that a new projecting building adjacent has now made it impossible to see the course fully from the balcony.

THE RIVER FOWEY in Cornwall has its tree-lined banks wide apart at Golant. Here may be found the unpretentious boathouse of **Castle Dore** RC, a simple corrugated shed once used for boatbuilding. But the circumstances of the club's beginnings are somewhat complex.

In 1974 a group of enthusiasts started rowing in an ancient

*Castle Dore rows from Golant, a small place picturesquely sited on the River Fowey. The boathouse is unpretentious, and the approach road not without its own concerns, for a notice on the pole in the centre of the drawing declares 'Road liable to flooding. Do not leave your car unattended.'*

*These drawings show the Fowey Head of the River race course. It is at the King of Prussia that the competitors receive their reward, and there could not be a better place to aim at. The scene has characteristic Cornish charm: the church of St Fimbarrus on one side of the inn, and Place, the 1457 Seat of the Treffry family, on the other. Town Quay itself is worth rowing for. Incidentally, there is evidence that Kenneth Grahame was inspired to write the opening chapter of 'The Wind in the Willows' after making a boating excursion from Fowey to Golant, for he often visited this river with his friends Arthur Quiller-Couch and the redoubtable sculler F.J. Furnivall.*

Clinker four and clearly found such craft more interesting than the new, for they took part in rowing a replica Viking longship across the bay of St Ives. Having earned some travelling expenses from the sponsor, what better than start a rowing club? Soon it was participating in the Tideway Head, the Veterans' Tideway Head, most of the West of England regattas and its own Fowey head.

The 4½-mile course begins by St Winnow, passes Golant and ends at Fowey itself, near the Town Quay and, most important, the King of Prussia, where the trophies are presented. The club makes use of other hostelries too: its own Golant Fisherman's Arms acts as clubhouse.

Hopes are high for the future: an entry to the Royal Fowey Regatta, its own invitation regatta. The club was represented at the ARA Centenary Pageant in 1982 with a Thames skiff and a West of England four including three generations in its crew.

For a club founded as recently as 1981, it has achieved much. But even the youngest have some history: the name Castle Dor derives from an Iron Age ring fort nearby. Perhaps the boats will be called after the legendary King Mark or Tristram and Iseult.

FALMOUTH HAS BEEN IMPORTANT since the seventeenth century,

*Falmouth is a busy port, and the inner harbour the centre of shipping. But apart from the docks and jetties, so often berthing large ships, there is the sailing and rowing which uses the area around the Town Quay, Grove Place. As these drawings show, Greenbank Falmouth rowing club has no impressive boathouse, but its shared Nissen hut enjoys a waterside position and it is from here that the regatta takes place in the harbour.*

*The view from the St Andrews suspension bridge looking upstream has the King's, or George V, Bridge at the sharp bend, and the massive boathouse which accommodates Glasgow RC, Glasgow Schools and Glasgow University clubs.*

when a mail-packet station was set up. As the third largest natural harbour in the world, only Sydney and Rio de Janeiro exceeding it, this sheltered water has fostered recreation as well as commerce.

Although **Greenbank Falmouth** RC dates only from 1972, its direct ancestor, the Greenbank Aquatic Club was involved for many years in Cornish rowing. This aspect of the sport is quite distinct, having its own regatta circuit and type of boat with fixed seat. To complicate matters further, there are also the traditional Newquay and Isle of Scilly gigs, pilot cutters often over a hundred years old. These coxed sixes are still to be seen in one race on the Fal.

However, Greenbank concentrates on the conventional rowing, holding a regatta each year in the harbour, where the course may vary annually. The setting is that of the inner harbour with the three jetties, Queen's, Empire and King's, and Duchy Wharf on one side, while on the other the water front of the town leads to Penryn further up river.

The boathouse is just an old Nissen hut and is surrounded by other 'temporary' structures, but that does not seem to matter to a club which has been West of England champion in five out of eight seasons.

# CHAPTER FOURTEEN

## *Scotland*

### GLASGOW · CLYDE · LOCH LOMOND · NITHSDALE

ALMOST FROM THE START of the sport of rowing in Scotland, the Clyde has been its major cradle, with the clubs and regattas the chief nurses. With the now defunct Dumbarton Regatta on the Clyde, inaugurated in 1829, racing in the harbour lasted till the 1970s fund-raising events in jollyboats. However, the traditional skills of jollyboat racing continue at the regattas held by the **Royal West of Scotland** ABC at Greenock, and at Port Bannatyne, Isle of Bute.

The first Glasgow-based club, **Clydesdale** ARC, was founded 1857, and the local governing body grew from the Glasgow and West of Scotland ARA to become the national Scottish ARA.

Of the educational establishments on the river, **Glasgow University** BC records show only that it was formed before 1877, **Strathclyde University** BC in the 1960s, and in 1942 a joint **Glasgow Schools** RC was established to share facilities.

Incidentally, the famous football clubs of Glasgow, Rangers and Clyde, owe their existence to the rowing clubs.

In the 1920s many trades clubs came into prominence as an alternative to the 'gentlemen amateurs'; those whose origins went back before the turn of the century included Glasgow Printers and Newark, one of several clubs from the 'tail o' the bank' part of the Clyde estuary that witnessed the sailing of the great Cunard Queens. However, in 1947 both kinds of club amalgamated.

SINCE THE END of World War II the Clyde has remained prominent in Scottish rowing, although many of the coastal clubs either failed to re-establish themselves or gradually faded away. The consequent move of the sport into fine shells made life difficult for the followers of the jollyboat traditions.

Within Glasgow, the Clyde was host to the various Scottish championships when they were individual events, and even when they were organized into one Championship Regatta. But increasing sophistication moved the championships to the straight multi-lane courses, at first Lochwinnoch and then Strathclyde Park. Consequently the only championship event Clyde still hosts is that

*Glasgow Green lies at the heart of that city, its wooded area bordering the Clyde. Here the river has a straight between St Andrews and the Victoria and Albert Bridges, all three of which can be seen in the drawing, while just before Albert Bridge the Clydesdale boathouse hugs the north bank overlooking a weir. Prominent in the background are the Merchant's Steeple, Bridegate, of 1665 and the tower of the Central Station Hotel, 1884.*

*Strathclyde Country Park, some 1,650 acres of countryside in the valley of the River Clyde between Hamilton and Motherwell, was opened in 1978. One of its most important features is the man-made Strathclyde Loch running almost the whole length of the park. The 2,000-metre rowing course, with six lanes, together with the fine Centre, has international standard events and can consider itself the national rowing centre of Scotland. The drawing includes the Watersports Centre at the southern end of the loch with its excellent spectator accommodation as well as boat storage beneath.*

in jollyboat fours at Greenock.

Nevertheless, it should not be supposed that the Clyde is deprived of regattas; on the contrary, almost half the racing in the Scottish calendar is held on this river. The first Head of the River race in coxed fours was started in the 1950s by Clydesdale, and the Clyde Rowing Weekend has grown into one of the biggest regattas in Britain.

FURTHER SOUTH, developments were taking place as early as 1838; as the *Dumfries and Galloway Courier* reported: 'In Kirkcudbright and elsewhere amateur boating has for some time been practised and is encouraged and appreciated. Last autumn witnessed the first gig upon the Nith ... the glorious sweep from the New Bridge to Albany Place will oft in future times be redolent of that life and animation which is imparted to it by the contests of the boatmen.'

There is no reason to suppose that the Dumfries Regatta was any less attractive than the Kirkcudbright one. Indeed, today the **Nithsdale** ARC can look back on a number of noteworthy successes, not least that of Dumfries Academy's coxed four which won the British Championship in 1969, despite using a shell-boat made by Sims of Putney at the turn of the century for the Howard family of Brampton in Cumberland. But then Nithsdale has an interest in its past, for its first regatta was in 1837; its first Commodore, Sir James Anderson, experimented with an all-metal rowing boat on the Nith before he captained Brunel's *Great Eastern* across the Atlantic, leaving to his club its oldest trophy, a silver gig; and an early member, a former pupil at Dumfries Academy, was Sir James Barrie.

BUT IT IS NOT only on firth or river that Scottish rowing can be seen. The loch also hosts the sport, and of them all perhaps **Loch Lomond** RC, founded in 1827, has the most beautiful setting. The earliest recorded competition took place in the following year, and regattas have been held there ever since, nowadays attracting crowds greater than anywhere else except perhaps Henley.

The club is based at the southern end of the Loch, on the River Leven, its boathouse only ten years old. Over the years the regatta has been held on a number of sites, hardly surprising on the largest stretch of inland water in Britain. The first course was $2\frac{1}{2}$ miles, followed by a shorter mile and a quarter, used for many Scottish championships until the opening of Strathclyde Park. A third course, for most of the big professional races from 1880 to 1913, ran to the piers at Balloch, from which the loch steamers sailed, while the present course is on the east side at Balloch Castle Park. With the exception of a course up in the Straits of Luss, all these are prone to a crosswind. Consequently many regattas were disrupted with

*There has been organized rowing on Loch Lomond since 1828, though regatta courses have moved five times from one part of this, the largest stretch of water on the mainland, to another. Most of the activity was on the west side of the loch, but today the eastern part is preferred. This drawing shows the superb view from Balloch Castle Park to the regatta centre. To the left the River Leven joins the loch, and it is there that the rowing club has its base.*

boats sinking – on one occasion an eight broke in half, and the stern four, unaware of what had happened, rowed on only to be passed by the bow four, who were swimming for the shore. But then there have been numerous incidents: in 1894 the water level was so low that a crew ran aground in the middle of the course, and a sculler who fell in almost at the finishing line was disqualified for 'walking his boat over the line'!

# APPENDIX I

## The Clubs affiliated to the Amateur Rowing Association, March 1985

*The date is the year of foundation.*

ABINGDON RC. 1958. *Oarblade:* Green and yellow. *Singlet:* Yellow. *Boathouse:* Wilsham Road.

AGECROFT RC. 1861. *Oarblade:* Red and white on blue. *Singlet:* Red and white. *Boathouse:* Littleton Road, Salford 7.

ALPHA WOMEN'S AMATEUR RC. 1927. (*See also Mortlake, Anglian and Alpha*). *Oarblade:* Black, white and orange. *Singlet:* Black, with orange and white hoops.

ALTON BLADES RC. *Oarblade:* Turquoise, white and scarlet. *Singlet:* White with turquoise and scarlet badge. *Boathouse:* Alton Water.

ANCHOLME RC. 1868. Re-established 1970. *Oarblade:* White and dark blue cross pattee. *Singlet:* White and dark blue hoops. *Boathouse:* Manley Gardens, Brigg, South Humberside.

ARA NATIONAL SQUAD. 1975. *Oarblade:* White, blue collar, red tip. *Singlet:* White with red and blue hoops. *Boathouse:* 6 Lower Mall, Hammersmith, London W6.

ARTHUR ANDERSON RC. 1981. *Oarblade:* Red, black and white. *Singlet:*

Blue. *Boathouse:* G.B. Battersby, Cookham, 1 Surrey Street, London WC2.

ATHENA LADIES RC. 1977. *Oarblade:* White, with blue and green chevrons. *Singlet:* White. *Boathouse:* The Groves, Chester.

AURIOL KENSINGTON RC. 1981, by amalgamation of Kensington RC (1872) and Auriol RC (1896). *Colours:* Pink and green. *Boathouse:* 14 Lower Mall, Hammersmith, London W6.

AVON COUNTY RC. 1972, by amalgamation of Avon RC (1865) and Bristol RC (1961). *Colours:* Black and amber. *Boathouse:* Saltford.

BARCLAYS BANK RC. 1936. *Oarblade:* Black with maroon, silver and gold bands. *Singlet:* White, with black, maroon, silver and gold hoops. *Boathouse:* Embankment, Putney, London SW15.

BASS RC. 1976. *Oarblade:* Plain white. *Singlet:* Nut brown, flame red, orange. *Boathouse:* Burton Leander RC, The Boathouse, Stapenhill Road, Burton-on-Trent, Staffs.

BATH, CITY OF, ARC. 1977. *Colours:*

Black and white bars. *Boathouse:* Bath Boating Station, Forester Road, Bathwick, Bath.

BEDFORD RC. 1886. *Oarblade:* Maroon and white or either of these. *Boathouse:* Duck Mill Lane, Bedford.

BEDFORD LRC. 1955. *Oarblade:* White, blue spline, maroon collar. *Singlet:* Royal blue. *Boathouse:* Star Club, Batts Ford, Commercial Road, Bedford.

BERWICK ARC. 1869. *Oarblade:* Royal blue, two white chevrons. *Singlet:* White, trimmed royal blue. *Boathouse:* New Road, Berwick-on-Tweed, Northumberland.

BEWDLEY RC. 1877. *Oarblade:* Blue and gold. *Singlet:* Indigo blue with gold band. *Boathouse:* Severnside North, Wribbenhall.

BEWL BRIDGE RC. 1977. *Boathouse:* Bewl Bridge Reservoir, Lamberhurst, Kent.

BEXHILL RC. 1890. *Colours:* Red, white and green. *Boathouse:* The Colonade, Bexhill-on-Sea.

BIDEFORD AAC. 1870. *Oarblade:* Light blue. *Singlet:* Light blue and white. *Boathouse:* The Pill, Bideford, Devon.

BIDEFORD ARC. 1882. *Oarblade and Singlet:* Red. *Boathouse:* The Quay, Bideford, Devon.

BIRMINGHAM RC. 1873. *Oarblade:* White, with dark blue collar and triangle at tip. *Singlet:* Dark blue with white hoop. *Boathouse:* Edgbaston Reservoir, Reservoir Road, Edgbaston, Birmingham 16.

BLYTH RC. 1874. *Oarblade:* Dark blue, white collar and tip. *Singlet:* Dark blue, two white diagonals. *Boathouse:* South Harbour, Blyth, Northumberland.

BOSTON RC. 1856. *Oarblade:* Blue. *Singlet:* Blue with white hoop. *Boathouse:* Carlton Road, Boston, Lincs.

BRADFORD ARC. 1867. *Oarblade:* Dark blue and white diagonal stripes. *Singlet:* Dark blue. *Boathouse:* Hirst Weir, Shipley.

BRADFORD-ON-AVON RC. 1873. *Oarblade:* White, with scarlet bar. *Singlet:* White, with two scarlet bands. *Boathouse:* Barton Bridge, Pound Lane, Bradford-on-Avon.

BRIDGNORTH RC

BRIGHTON CRUISING CLUB. 1892. *Oarblade:* Blue, with gold tip. *Singlet:* Blue, with gold band. *Boathouse:* 173-178 Kings Road Arches, Brighton.

BRISTOL ARIEL RC. 1870. *Boathouse:* White with Oxford blue, Maltese cross. *Singlet:* White, trimmed Oxford blue. *Boathouse:* Birchwood, St Annes, Bristol 4.

BRITANNIA RC. 1894. *Now part Lea RC.*

BRITISH AIRWAYS CLUBS ROWING SECTION. 1973. *Oarblade:* Red white and blue. *Singlet:* Red. *Boathouse:* Staines BC.

BRITISH TRANSPORT COMMISSION (SOUTHAMPTON) RC. 1927. *Oarblade:* Blue, two white bars. *Singlet:* Blue with white band. *Boathouse:* No. 4 Berth, Southampton East Docks.

BROCAS CLUB, THE. 1962. *Oarblade:* Dark blue. *Singlet:* White.

BROXBOURNE RC. 1860. *Oarblade:* Light blue. *Singlet:* White with light and dark blue diagonal. *Boathouse:* Old Nazeing Road, Broxbourne, Herts.

BURTON LEANDER RC. 1847. *Oarblade:* White, red and black. *Singlet:* Red or white. *Boathouse:* Stapenhill Road, Burton-on-Trent.

BURWAY RC. 1921. *Oarblade:* Gold and dark blue. *Singlet:* Yellow. *Boathouse:* Thameside, Laleham-on-Thames.

CAMBOIS ARC. 1911. *Oarblade:* Green and white triangle. *Singlet:* Green. *Boathouse:* River Blyth.

CAMBRIDGE, CITY OF, RC. 1863. *Oarblade:* Dark blue, a claret band within two old gold bands. *Singlet:* Dark blue. *Boathouse:* Riverside, via Kimberley Road, Cambridge.

CAMBRIDGE '99 RC. 1899. *Oarblade:*

Light blue with dark green band, old gold tip. *Singlet:* Light blue. *Boathouse:* Via Kimberley Road, Cambridge.

CAMBRIDGE TELEPHONES RC. 1971. *Oarblade and Singlet:* Blue. *Boathouse:* CRA, River Cam, Cambridge.

CANTABRIGIAN RC. 1950. *Oarblade:* Dark blue and silver. *Singlet:* White, trimmed blue. *Boathouse:* Banhams Middle Yard, Cambridge.

CASTLE DORE RC. 1974. *Oarblade and Singlet:* Purple and white. *Boathouse:* Quayside, Golant, Fowey, Cornwall.

CHRISTCHURCH RC. 1948. *Oarblade:* Blue, gold, green, longitudinally. *Singlet:* Gold with single blue and green hoops. *Boathouse:* Wick Lane, Christchurch, Dorset.

CITY OF BRISTOL RC. 1962. *Colours:* Green. *Boathouse:* Welsh Back, Bristol.

CITY ORIENT RC. 1934. *Now part of Lea RC.*

CIVIL SERVICE LRC. 1927. *Oarblade:* Blue and white. *Singlet:* White with blue hoops. *Boathouse:* Civil Service Boathouse, Dukes Meadow, London W4.

COLET BC. *Oarblade:* Black back, white front, red tip. *Singlet:* White, trimmed black, white and red. *Boathouse:* St Paul's School, London SW13.

COMBINED SERVICES RC. 1980. *Oarblade:* Navy blue and sky blue. *Singlet:* Scarlet.

CRESCENT RC. *Singlet:* Green, blue and gold. *Boathouse:* Spring Hill, Clapton, London E5.

CROWLAND RC. 1939. *Now part of Lea RC.*

CURLEW RC. 1866. *Oarblade:* Dark blue, light blue and white. *Singlet:* Dark blue. *Boathouse:* Crane Street, London SE10.

CYGNET RC. 1890. *Oarblade:* Light blue with dark blue diagonal. *Singlet:* Light and dark blue. *Boathouse:* Civil Service Boathouse, Dukes Meadows, London W4.

DACRE BC. 1961. *Oarblade:* Red and silver. *Singlet:* Red. *Boathouse:* Emanuel School Boathouse, Dukes Meadows, Chiswick, London W4.

DART ARC. About 1861. *Oarblade and Singlet:* Black. *Boathouse:* Baltic Wharf, Totnes, Devon.

DARTMOUTH ARC. 1869. *Oarblade and Singlet:* White. *Boathouse:* Sandquay Road, Dartmouth.

DEAL, WALMER AND KINGSDOWN RC. 1927. *Oarblade:* Purple and grey. *Singlet:* Purple with grey sash. *Boathouse:* The Marina, Deal, Kent.

DERBY RC. 1879. *Oarblade and Singlet:* White with red, black and Cambridge blue bands. *Boathouse:* Darley Grove, Derby.

DERWENT RC. 1857. *Oarblade:* Cambridge blue (front) and Oxford blue (reverse). *Singlet:* White, trimmed with above colours. *Boathouse:* Darley Grove, Derby.

DOVER RC. 1846. *Oarblade:* Blue and white stripes. *Singlet:* Royal blue with white band. *Boathouse:* East Cliff, Dover.

DURHAM AMATEUR RC. 1860. *Oarblade:* Dark blue, a gold chevron. *Singlet:* Gold, trimmed dark blue. *Boathouse:* Greenlane, The Racecourse, Durham.

EASTBOURNE RC

ERITH RC. 1942. *Oarblade:* Green, with white 'E'. *Singlet:* Green, two white diagonals. *Boathouse:* Riversite, Erith.

ETON EXCELSIOR RC. 1851. *Oarblade:* Blue with amber bar. *Singlet:* Blue with amber hoop. *Boathouse:* King Stable Street, Eton, Windsor, Berks.

ETON MISSION RC. 1885. *Oarblade:* White. *Singlet:* White, trimmed light blue. *Boathouse:* Johnstone Boathouse, 127 Wallis Road, Hackney Wick, London E9.

ETON VIKINGS. 1897.

EVESHAM RC. 1863. *Oarblade:* Dark blue and white. *Singlet:* Dark blue, trimmed white. *Boathouse:* Abbey Park, Evesham, Worcs.

EXETER RC. 1946. *Successor to Exeter ARC (1864) and Port Royal ARC (1972). Oarblade:* Green, white spear. *Singlet:* Bottle green, with white trim.

EYRE CLUB. 1968. *Oarblade:* Plain, with red, black and white band. *Singlet:* White or white trimmed colours. *Boathouse:* Thames RC.

FALCON RC. 1869. *Oarblade:* Amber with blue and black chevrons. *Singlet:* Blue, black and amber. *Boathouse:* Meadow Lane (off Iffley Road), Oxford.

FAWLEY WAY BC. 1971. *Oarblade:* Red, white, black, *Singlet:* White, with black trim. *Boathouse:* Thames RC.

FOLKESTONE RC. 1852. *Oarblade:* Yellow, black strip. *Singlet:* Yellow. *Boathouse:* The Parade, Sandgate, Folkestone.

FOSSE SCULLING CLUB. 1983. *Oarblade:* Plain. *Singlet:* Maroon. *Boathouse:* Batheaston, 'Bramblegot', Bremhill, Calne, Wiltshire.

FREE PRESS BC. 1979. *Oarblade:* Black-tipped, white diagonally. *Singlet:* Black. *Boathouse:* Victoria Bridge, c/o Christ's College, Cambridge.

FULHAM RC. 1982. *Oarblade:* Black, with green stripe. *Singlet:* Black, with green sripe. *Boathouse:* Star & Garter Mansions.

FURNIVALL ScC. 1896. *Oarblade:* Myrtle and old gold on white. *Singlet:* Myrtle and old gold hoops on white. *Boathouse:* 19 Lower Mall, London W6.

GAINSBOROUGH RC. 1863. *Oarblade:* Blue and white Maltese cross. *Singlet:* Blue, trimmed white. *Boathouse:* 20 Caskgate Street, Gainsborough, Lincs.

GLADSTONE WARWICK RC. 1958. *Now part of Lea RC.*

GLOBE RC. 1923. *Oarblade:* Blue with white diagonal stripe. *Singlet:* White, trimmed blue, with blue hoop.

*Boathouse:* Trafalgar Rowing Centre, Crane Street, Greenwich, London SE10.

GLOUCESTER RC. 1846. *Oarblade and Singlet:* Black, with red and white diagonal. *Boathouse:* Gloucester Boathouse, Bristol Road, Hempsted, Gloucester.

GRABURN WAY RC. 1978. *Oarblade:* Black with white spot. *Singlet:* White and black. *Boathouse:* Molesey BC, Barge Walk, East Molesey, Surrey.

GRANTA BOAT CLUB. 1983. *Oarblade:* Cambridge blue. *Singlet:* Cambridge blue. *Boathouse:* Trinity Boathouse, River Cam, 254 Mill Road, Cambridge.

GRAVESEND RC. 1878. *Oarblade:* Dark red on a white band and a light red bar. *Singlet:* Dark red. *Boathouse:* New Bridge, Gravesend, Kent.

GRAY'S INN BOAT CLUB. 1983. *Oarblade:* Silver gold maroon blue. *Singlet:* Blue with silver griffon. *Boathouse:* Duck Mill Lane, Bedford.

GREENBANK FALMOUTH RC. 1972. *Oarblade:* Red with white collar and spoon. *Singlet:* White with two red bands. *Boathouse:* Grove Place, Falmouth.

GROSVENOR RC, 1869. *Oarblade:* Dark blue, two orange bars. *Singlet:* Orange. *Boathouse:* The Groves, Chester.

GUILDFORD RC. 1880. *Oarblade:* Green, two gold bars. *Singlet:* Green. *Boathouse:* Shalford Road, Guildford, Surrey.

HASTINGS ARC. 1979. *Oarblade and Singlet:* Red and yellow.

HEFFALUMP BC. 1973. *Oarblade and Singlet:* White with maroon/light blue/black diagonal. *Boathouse:* Holme Pierrepont National Water Sports Centre, Nottingham.

HENLEY RC. 1839. *Oarblade:* Dark blue, white collar. *Singlet:* White, trimmed dark blue. *Boathouse:* Riverside, Henley.

HEREFORD RC. 1860. *Oarblade:* Blue,

barred white and red. *Singlet:* White ringed blue, trimmed red. *Boathouse:* 37 Greyfriars Avenue, Hereford.

HERNE BAY ARC. 1887. *Oarblade and Singlet:* Blue with white Maltese cross. *Boathouse:* Hampton Beach, Herne Bay.

HEXHAM BC. 1878. *Oarblade:* Yellow with brown tip, blue cross. *Singlet:* Yellow. *Boathouse:* Tyne Green, Hexham.

HOLLINGWORTH LAKE RC. 1872. *Oarblade:* Royal blue/white parted diagonally. *Singlet:* Royal blue/white. *Boathouse:* Smithy Bridge, Littleborough. Lancs.

HORSEFERRY RC. 1938. *Oarblade:* Plain with red, blue and old gold chevrons. *Singlet:* Red with blue and gold hoops. *Boathouse:* Kew Bridge Road, Brentford, Middlesex.

HUNTINGDON BC. 1854. *Oarblade:* Cardinal red and dark blue. *Singlet:* Cardinal red with dark blue diagonal. *Boathouse:* Mill Common, Huntingdon, Cambs.

IBIS RC. 1871. *Oarblade:* Blue with yellow and red diagonal or a scarlet ibis. *Singlet:* Blue with yellow and red diagonals or white. *Boathouse:* Hartington Road, London W4.

IRONBRIDGE RC. 1870. *Oarblade:* Green with gold tip. *Singlet:* Green and gold. *Boathouse:* Coalbrookdale (River Severn).

JOHN O'GAUNT RC. 1866. *Oarblade:* Blue with gold bar. *Singlet:* White with blue and gold hoops. *Boathouse:* Halton Road, Skerton.

KINGSTON RC. 1858. *Oarblade:* Scarlet and white. *Singlet:* Scarlet and white. *Boathouse:* Canbury Gardens, Lower Ham Road, Kingston-upon-Thames, Surrey.

KINGSTON RC (HULL). 1882. *Oarblade:* Royal blue, two white chevrons. *Singlet:* Royal blue, trimmed white. *Boathouse:* Oak Road Playing Fields, Beresford Avenue, Hull.

LADY VICTORIA 1969 BC. 1983.

LEA RC. 1980. *Oarblade and Singlet:* Orange. *Boathouse:* The Boathouse, Spring Hill, Clapton, London E5.

LEANDER CLUB. 1818. *Oarblade:* Cerise. *Singlet:* White with club emblem. *Boathouse:* Henley-on-Thames, Oxon.

LEICESTER RC. 1882. *Oarblade:* Black and white. *Singlet:* White and black stripe and trim. *Boathouse:* The Bedehouse, Upperton Road, Leicester.

LENSBURY RC. 1921. *Oarblade:* Chevronry black and orange, tipped purple. *Singlet:* Orange. *Boathouse:* Embankment, Putney, London SW15.

LEVIATHAN BC. 1959, re-formed 1972. *Oarblade:* White. *Singlet:* White with blue whale. *Boathouse:* The Lodge, Fenside, Catfield, Great Yarmouth, Norfolk.

LIVERPOOL VICTORIA RC. 1884. *Oarblade:* Claret tip. *Singlet:* Claret, trimmed gold. *Boathouse:* West Float, Birkenhead.

LONDON RC. 1856. *Oarblade:* Two blue bands with white bars. *Singlet:* White, trimmed in club colours and/or flag. *Boathouse:* Embankment, Putney, London SW15.

LONDON SCOTTISH RC.

LONDON TRANSPORT (CRS) (GREENWICH) RC. 1946. *Oarblade:* Blue and amber. *Singlet:* White, a blue and amber band. *Boathouse:* Curlew RC, Crane Street, London SE10.

LONDON TRANSPORT (CRS) (LEA) RC. ———. *Colours:* Royal blue and amber.

LONDON TRANSPORT (CRS) (THAMES) RC. 1930 *Oarblade:* Blue and amber. *Singlet:* Blue and amber hoops. *Boathouse:* The Priory, 6 Lower Mall, Hammersmith, London.

LONDON TRANSPORT (DISTRICT LINE) RC 1912 *Oarblade:* Light blue, dark blue, light blue chevrons *singlet:* light blue with dark blue band *Boathouse:* 6 Lower Mall, Hammersmith, London.

LONDON WELSH RC. 1982. *Oarblade:* Red dragon. *Singlet:* Scarlet. *Boathouse:* Putney.

LOUGHBOROUGH BC. 1881 (*Re-established 1948*). *Oarblade and Singlet:* Blue and old gold. *Boathouse:* County Bridge, Loughborough.

LOWESTOFT RC. 1977. *Oarblade:* Dark blue with two light blue bands. *Singlet:* Light blue. *Boathouse:* Oulton Broad, Lowestoft.

LYMINGTON ARC. 1948. *Oarblade:* Sky-blue with maroon band. *Singlet:* Sky-blue with maroon band. *Boathouse:* Quay Road, Lymington, Hants.

MACKNEY-BROOK SCULLING CLUB. 1981. *Oarblade:* White/blue tip. *Singlet:* Red and blue. *Boathouse:* Thames Street, Wallingford, Oxon.

MAIDENHEAD RC. 1876. *Oarblade:* Dark green with green star in white circle. *Singlet:* Dark green, trimmed white, green star on white ground. *Boathouse:* Maidenhead Bridge.

MARLOW RC. 1871. *Oarblade:* Cardinal. *Singlet:* White, trimmed cardinal. *Boathouse:* Marlow Bridge.

MEDWAY TOWNS RC. 1958. (*Amalgamating Medway and Chatham and Gillingham RCs (1865)*). *Oarblade:* Red and amber with white horse badge. *Singlet:* Red and amber hoop. *Boathouse:* Esplanade, Rochester. Kent.

MERCIA SCULLERS. 1970. *Oarblade and Singlet:* Orange with black diagonal. *Boathouse:* Bewdley.

METROPOLITAN RC. 1964. *Colours:* White and blue. C/o London RC. Embankment, London SW15.

METROPOLITAN POLICE RC. 1964. *Colours:* Blue, gold and silver. *Rowing Centres:* Poplar, Kingston.

MIDLAND BANK RC. 1878. *Oarblade and Singlet:* Chocolate, green and gold. *Boathouse:* Embankment, London SW15.

MOLESEY BC. 1866. *Oarblade:* Black. *Singlet:* White. *Boathouse:* Barge Walk, East Molesey, Surrey.

MORTLAKE ANGLIAN & ALPHA BC. —. *Oarblade:* White with geranium and black diagonal bands. *Singlet:* Geranium and black diagonal bands on white. *Boathouse:* Kew Meadows Path, Richmond, Surrey.

NATIONAL WESTMINSTER BANK RC. 1968. (*From amalgamation of National Provincial Bank RC (1884) and Westminster Bank RC (1906).*) *Oarblade:* Dark blue with light blue and cerise. *Singlet:* Dark blue, trimmed cerise, light blue diagonals. *Boathouse:* The Embankment, Putney, London SW15.

NATIVES BOAT CLUB. 1983. *Oarblade:* Natural, with pink, black and blue band. *Colours:* White zephyr trimmed with pink, black and blue. *Boathouse:* Hounslow Borough Boathouse, Barnes Bridge.

NAUTILUS LIGHTWEIGHT RC. 1963. *Oarblade:* White, blue collar, red tip. *Singlet:* White with red and blue hoop. C/o Amateur Rowing Association, 6 Lower Mall, London W6.

NEPTUNE RC. 1882 (*disbanded 1937, re-established 1975*). *Oarblade:* Maroon with gold bands at blade end and loom neck. *Singlet:* Maroon. *Boathouse:* Ferry Lane, Kings Lynn, Norfolk.

NEWARK RC. 1873. *Oarblade:* Cardinal red with navy blue tip and collar. *Singlet:* White, trimmed colours. *Boathouse:* Farndon Road, Newark, Notts.

NEWT SCULLERS. 1983. *Oarblade:* Yellow with cerise and green stripes. *Singlet:* Yellow. *Boathouse:* Newark RC.

NOMAD BC. 1979. *Oarblade and Singlet:* Black, with orange and light blue hoops.

NORTH STAFFS RC. 1970. *Oarblade:* Green with gold Staffordshire knot. *Singlet:* Green. *Boathouse:* Chalet Boathouse, Trentham Gardens, Newcastle-under-Lyme, Staffs.

NORTHAMPTON RC. 1976. *Oarblade:* Amber and black. *Singlet:* Amber and black diagonal stripes. *Boathouse:* Rush

Mills House, Bedford Road, Northampton.

NORTHWICH RC. 1875. *Oarblade:* Green and gold halved. *Singlet:* Gold with green band. *Boathouse:* The Crescent, Riverside, Northwich, Cheshire.

NORWICH RC. 1973. *Oarblade and Singlet:* Green and yellow. *Boathouse:* Whitlingham Lane, Trowse, Norwich.

NORWICH UNION RC. 1905. *Oarblade:* Green and silver. *Singlet:* White. *Boathouse:* Thorpe St Andrew (River Yare).

NOTTINGHAM BC. 1894. *Oarblade:* Royal blue, gold collar. *Singlet:* Royal blue. *Boathouse:* Middle of Three, Trentside. Trent Bridge, West Bridgford, Nottingham.

NOTTINGHAMSHIRE COUNTY ROWING ASSOCIATION. 1981. *Colours:* Green and yellow. *Boathouse:* National Water Sports Centre, Holme Pierrepont.

NOTTINGHAM & UNION RC 1862. *Oarblade*: Black and crimson. *Singlet*: Crimson. *Boathouse*: Trent Bridge.

NOTTINGHAM BRITANNIA RC. 1869. *Oarblade:* Dark and light blue. *Singlet:* Dark blue, club badge on chest. *Boathouse:* Trent Bridge.

OPTIMISTS, THE. 1970. The Rowing Registrar, 3 Churton Place, London SW1.

ORANGE BC. 1969. *Oarblade and Singlet:* Orange.

OXFORD, CITY OF, RC. 1968. *Amalgamation of former Hannington and Neptune RC's.* *Oarblade:* Oxford blue, red with white bar. *Singlet:* Oxford blue, red and white. *Boathouse:* City Boathouse, Meadow Lane, Oxford.

PAIGNTON ARC. ——. *Oarblade:* Old gold with royal blue bar. *Singlet:* Old gold with royal blue diagonal. *Boathouse:* The Harbour, South Quay, Paignton, Devon.

PENGWERN BC. 1871. *Oarblade:* Dark

blue. *Singlet:* Blue and gold. *Boathouse:* Kingsland, Shrewsbury.

PETERBOROUGH CITY RC. ——. *Oarblade:* White, royal blue and old gold bands. *Singlet:* White, royal blue and old gold bands (ringed). *Boathouse:* Thorpe Meadows, Thorpe Road, Peterborough.

PHOENIX. 1983. *Colours:* As University of London WBC.

PLYMOUTH ARC. 1949. *Oarblade:* White with one broad black and narrow green bands either side. *Singlet:* White with green and black bands. *Boathouse:* Arnolds Point, Laira, Plymouth.

POOLE ARC. 1873. *Oarblade:* White with red tip. *Singlet:* White with one red loop. *Boathouse:* 1 West Quay Road, Poole, Dorset.

POPLAR, BLACKWALL & DISTRICT RC. 1845. *Oarblade:* White with amber and black stripes. *Singlet:* White with amber and black hoops. *Boathouse:* Ferry Street, Cubitt Town. London E14.

PUTNEY TOWN RC. 1922. *Oarblade:* Dark blue with white bar. *Singlet:* Dark blue, trimmed white. *Boathouse:* Dukes Head Hotel, Lower Richmond Road, Putney.

QUINTIN BC. 1907. *Oarblade and Singlet:* Dark blue, two white diagonals. *Boathouse:* Polytechnic Boathouse, Hartington Road, London W4.

RADLEY MARINERS. 1962. (*1925 as Old Radleian BC*). *Colours:* Cerise and white. *Boathouse:* Radley College.

RATS CLUB. ——. The Boathouse. Batts Ford, Commercial Road, Bedford.

READING RC. 1867. *Oarblade and Singlet:* Blue on white. *Boathouse:* Caversham Bridge.

RENTACREW RC. 1972.

REX BC. 1981. *Oarblade:* White, with blue and green chevrons. *Singlet:* Bright green. *Boathouse:* King's School, Chester.

171

ROB ROY BC. 1880. *Oarblade:* White with Royal Irish maroon. *Singlet:* Royal Irish maroon. *Boathouse:* C.R.A. Boathouse, Kimberley Road, Cambridge.

ROSS RC. 1870. *Oarblade:* Claret, blue and white. *Singlet:* Claret with white and blue diagonals. *Boathouse:* Brooksmouth, Ross-on-Wye.

ROYAL AIR FORCE RC. 1947. *Oarblade:* Sky-blue with RAF roundel. *Singlet:* Sky-blue. *Boathouse:* Wallingford.

ROYAL CHESTER RC. 1838. *Oarblade:* Plain, a garter blue band. *Singlet:* Garter blue. *Boathouse:* The Groves, Chester.

ROYAL ENGINEERS RC. 1846 *Oarblade:* Red, three blue diagonal stripes. *Singlet:* Red, with three thin diagonal blue hoops.

ROYAL NAVY & ROYAL MARINES ARA. 1964. *Oarblade and Singlet:* Navy blue.

ROYAL NAVY RC (HMS HERON). 1964. *Oarblade:* Navy blue. *Singlet:* Yellow.

ROYAL NAVY RC (HMS FISGARD). 1964. *Oarblade and Singlet:* Navy blue/white. HMS Fisgard, Torpoint, East Cornwall.

ROYAL NAVY RC (HMS NEPTUNE). 1964. *Oarblade and Singlet:* Navy blue/white. HMS Neptune, Faslane, Helensburgh, Dunbartonshire.

ROYAL NAVY RC (ROYAL NAVAL ENGINEERING COLLEGE). 1964. *Oarblade and Singlet:* Navy blue/white. RNEC Manadon. Plymouth, Devon.

ROYAL NAVY RC (BRITANNIA ROYAL NAVAL COLLEGE). 1964. *Oarblade and Singlet:* Navy blue/white. BRNC. Dartmouth, Devon.

ROYAL NAVY, PORTSMOUTH, RC. 1965. *Oarblade:* Royal blue. *Singlet:* White. *Boathouse:* Hornsea Island, Portsmouth, Hants.

RUNCORN RC. 1894. *Oarblade:* Blue, two white bars. *Singlet:* Royal blue, two white bands. *Boathouse:* Rocksavage, Runcorn.

RYDE RC. 1877. *Oarblade:* Blue with yellow Maltese cross. *Singlet:* White with royal blue and gold hoops. *Boathouse:* Appley Park, Ryde, Isle of Wight.

ST GEORGE'S LADIES RC. ——. *Oarblade:* Red, white collar. *Singlet:* White, trimmed red.

ST IVES RC. 1860. *Oarblade:* Red and black. *Singlet:* Red. *Boathouse:* The Broadway, St Ives, Huntingdon, Cambs.

ST NEOTS RC. 1865. *Oarblade and Singlet:* Light blue with dark blue band. *Boathouse:* The Priory, St Neots, Huntingdon.

SABRINA CLUB. ——. *Colours:* Dark blue, chocolate and white.

SALTFORD RC. 1975. *Oarblade and Singlet:* Bands of equal width, dark blue, white, light blue. *Boathouse:* The Shallows, Saltford, Near Keynsham, Bristol.

SEAGULL RC. (*See Liverpool Victoria RC*).

SECOND ROYAL TANK REGIMENT RC. 1984.

SEFTON RC. 1958. *Oarblade:* Blue grass. *Singlet:* Light blue. *Boathouse:* Field Lane, Litherland, Liverpool.

SHANKLIN AND SANDOWN RC. 1875. *Oarblade and Singlet:* Royal blue. *Boathouse:* Esplanade, Shanklin, Isle of Wight.

SHEFFIELD, CITY OF, RC. 1968. *Oarblade:* Red, with silver tip. *Singlet:* Scarlet. *Boathouse:* Damflask Reservoir.

SHOREHAM RC. 1862. *Oarblade:* White with blue bar. *Singlet:* White with blue hoop. *Boathouse:* Kingston Beach, Shoreham, Sussex.

SKIFF CLUB. 1895. *Oarblade:* Plain, with amber and brown rings at neck. *Singlet:* Chocolate and gold. *Boathouse:* c/o Twickenham RC, Eel Pie Island, Twickenham, Middlesex.

SONS OF THE THAMES RC. 1886.

*Oarblade:* White with blue crossbars. *Singlet:* Royal blue and white. *Boathouse:* Hammersmith Boathouse, 28 Upper Mall, Hammersmith, London W6.

SOUTH HYLTON ARC. 1898. *Oarblade:* Light blue with three dark blue bars. *Singlet:* Light blue, trimmed dark blue. *Boathouse:* Waterside, South Hylton, Sunderland, Tyne and Wear.

SOUTHAMPTON ARC. 1945. *Oarblade:* Red and white quarters. *Singlet:* Red and white. *Boathouse:* Hazel Road, Woolston, Southampton.

SOUTHAMPTON COALPORTERS ARC. 1875. *Colours:* White, with black diamond. *Boathouse:* Northam Road, Northam, Southampton.

SOUTHSEA RC. 1860. *Oarblade:* Light blue, white, dark blue. *Singlet:* White. *Boathouse:* Clarence Beach, Southsea, Portsmouth.

SPHINX ROWING CLUB. 1974. *Oarblade:* Mediterranean blue two white bars and sphinx badge. *Singlet:* Blue. *Boathouse:* Canada Creek, West Float Birkenhead.

SPRINGHILL RC. 1972. Tyrells Boathouse, Spring Hill, London E5.

STAINES BC. (Before 1869). *Oarblade:* Dark green. *Singlet:* White, ringed green

STAR CLUB 1958. *Oarblade:* White with red star. *Singlet:* Sky blue, dark blue, scarlet and white. *Boathouse:* The Boathouse, Batts Ford, Commercial Road, Bedford.

STAR AND ARROW RC. 1980. *Oarblade:* Cerise. *Singlet:* White, with club emblem. *Boathouse:* C/o Leander Club, Henley-on-Thames, Oxon.

STOCK EXCHANGE RC. 1980. C/o London RC, Embankment, Putney, London SW15.

STOURPORT BC. 1876. *Oarblade:* Light and dark blue. *Singlet:* Light blue. *Boathouse:* Riverside (by bridge), Stourport-on-Severn.

STRATFORD-UPON-AVON BC.

1874. *Oarblade:* Crimson and black halved. *Singlet:* Crimson and black hoops. *Boathouse:* Recreation Ground, Stratford-upon-Avon.

STUART LADIES RC. 1949. *Now part of Lea RC.*

SUDBURY RC. 1874 *(as Stour BC—title changed 1975).* *Oarblade:* Oxford blue and white. *Singlet:* Oxford blue. *Boathouse:* Quay Lane, Sudbury, Suffolk.

TALKIN TARN ARC. 1859. *Oarblade:* Maroon and gold halved. *Singlet:* White. *Boathouse:* Talkin Tarn, Brampton, Cumbria.

TEES RC. 1864. *Oarblade:* Sky-blue, maroon tip. *Singlet:* Sky-blue, trimmed maroon. *Boathouse:* Boathouse Lane, Stockton-on-Tees.

THAMES RC. 1860. *Oarblade:* Plain with red, white and black band. *Singlet:* White with red, white and black. *Boathouse:* Embankment, Putney, London SW15.

THAMES TRADESMEN'S RC. 1896. *Oarblade:* Claret and green on white. *Singlet:* White with claret and green hoops. *Boathouse:* Kew Meadows Path, Kew, Richmond, Surrey.

TIDEWAY SCULLERS SCHOOL. 1958. *Oarblade:* Red and yellow diagonally. *Singlet:* Red and yellow bands. *Boathouse:* c/o Furnivall Sculling Club, 19 Lower Mall, Hammersmith W6.

TOFT RED LION RC. 1984.

TONBRIDGE BOARSMEN BC. 1981. *Oarblade:* Blue, with white boar's head. *Singlet:* White. *Boathouse:* River Medway, Tonbridge.

TORQUAY RC. 1869. *Oarblade:* Plain. *Singlet:* Blue with white hoop. *Boathouse:* Haldon Pier, Torquay.

TOWNMEAD RC. ——. *Oarblade and Singlet:* White.

TRAFFORD RC. 1957. *Oarblade and Singlet:* Black with white diagonal stripe. *Boathouse:* Dane Road, Sale.

TRENT RC. 1863. *Colours:* Blue and

white. *Boathouse:* Stapenhill Road, Burton-on-Trent.

TWICKENHAM RC. 1860. *Oarblade:* Plain, magenta and blue bands. *Singlet:* White with magenta and dark blue diagonal stripe. *Boathouse:* Eel Pie Island, Twickenham, Middlesex.

TYKES RC. 1984. *Oarblade:* Sky blue white rose.

TYNE RC. 1852. *Oarblade:* Black, two white bars. *Singlet:* Black. *Boathouse:* Riverside Boathouse, Newburn, Newcastle-upon-Tyne.

TYNEMOUTH RC. 1867. *Oarblade:* White, two blue bars. *Singlet:* White, two blue hoops. *Boathouse:* Priors Haven, Tynemouth.

UNITED UNIVERSITIES WBC. 1932. *Colours:* Red, black and white. *Boathouse:* Thames RC.

UNIVERSITY SPORTS BC *(formerly ACUA BC).*

UPPER THAMES RC. 1963. *Oarblade:* White. *Singlet:* Blue, white. *Boathouse:* Henley-on-Thames.

VAGA RC. ———. C/o Hereford RC, 37 Greyfriars Avenue, Hereford.

VESTA RC. 1870. *Oarblade:* White with crimson and black (oblique band). *Singlet:* White, one crimson and one black hoop. *Boathouse:* Embankment, Putney, London SW15.

VIGORNIA CLUB. 1841. *Oarblade and Singlet:* Light blue. *Boathouse:* Pitchcroft, Worcester.

WALBROOK RC. 1961. *Oarblade:* Green, yellow and black. *Singlet:* Green with black and yellow diagonal band. *Boathouse:* BP Boathouse, Trowlock Way, Teddington, Middlesex.

WALLINGFORD RC. 1947. *Oarblade and Singlet:* Scarlet and light blue. *Boathouse:* Thames Street, Wallingford.

WALTON RC. ———. *Oarblade:* Plain with light blue, dark blue, maroon chevrons. *Singlet:* White with light blue, dark blue and maroon hoops. *Boathouse:* Sunbury Lane, Walton-on-Thames, Surrey.

WARGRAVE BC. 1979. *Oarblade:* Grey, mid-blue and gold stripe. *Singlet:* Grey. *Boathouse:* 6 High Street, Wargrave, Berks.

WATFORD TOWN RC. 1984. *Colours:* Maroon and yellow.

WESTOVER AND BOURNE-MOUTH RC. 1865. *Oarblade:* White, red and black chevrons. *Singlet:* White with red and black hoop. *Boathouse:* West Beach, Bournemouth, Dorset.

WEYBRIDGE RC. 1880. *Oarblade:* Light blue, dark blue chevrons *Singlet:* Light blue with dark blue diagonal. *Boathouse:* Thames Lock, Jessamy Road, Weybridge, Surrey.

WEYBRIDGE LADIES ARC. 1926. *Oarblade:* Light blue, dark blue and scarlet bands. *Singlet:* Dark blue. *Boathouse:* Weybridge.

WHITBY FRIENDSHIP ARC. 1984. Don Wood, Club, New Way Ghaut. Church Street, Whitby, North Yorks

WHITE ROSE RC. 1979. *Oarblade:* White. *Singlet:* Black.

WORCESTER RC. 1874. *Oarblade:* Two black and one red band. *Singlet:* Black, edged scarlet, scarlet club motif on front. *Boathouse:* Pitchcroft, Worcester.

WORTHING RC. 1880. *Colours:* Red and blue stripes. *Boathouse:* Splash Point, Marine Parade, Worthing.

YARE BC. 1973. *Oarblade:* Banded blue and gold. *Singlet:* Blue. *Boathouse:* Thorpe, Norwich.

YORK CITY RC. 1863. *Oarblade and Singlet:* White with purple, black and gold diagonal. *Boathouse:* West Esplanade, Lendal Bridge, York.

*(Universities, Colleges and Hospitals)*

BALLIOL COLLEGE BC. ———. Balliol College, Oxford.

BATH UNIVERSITY RC. 1982. *Oarblade:* Black with yellow band. *Singlet:* Black with yellow hoop.

BIRMINGHAM UNIVERSITY RC.

174

1949. *Oarblade:* Light blue front, dark blue back. *Singlet:* White with black/-blue/red/horizontal bands. *Boathouse:* Edgbaston Reservoir.

BRADFORD, UNIVERSITY OF, BC. 1959 (*as Bradford Institute of Technology BC*). *Oarblade:* Black with red and white chevrons. *Singlet:* Black, trimmed white and red. *Boathouse:* Hirst Weir, Saltaire, Shipley.

BRASENOSE COLLEGE BC. ——. *Oarblade:* Black. *Singlet:* Black and yellow.

BRISTOL, UNIVERSITY OF, BC. 1909. *Oarblade:* Red and black. *Singlet:* White with black and red bands *or* black and red. *Boathouse:* River Avon, Saltford.

BRUNEL UNIVERSITY ROWING CLUB. 1983. *Oarblade:* Maroon and sky band. *Singlet:* white with maroon and sky bands

CAIUS BC. 1927. *Oarblade:* Black with light blue bar. *Singlet:* Light blue with white dove emblem. *Boathouse:* Pretoria Road, Gonville and Caius College, Cambridge.

CAMBRIDGE THEOLOGICAL COLLEGES' BC. 1982. *Oarblade:* White with red tips and bands. *Singlet:* White with red trim.

CAMBRIDGE UNIVERSITY BC. 1827. *Oarblade:* Light blue. *Singlet:* White, trimmed light blue, a lion emblem. *Boathouse:* Goldie Boathouse, Riverside, Kimberley Road, Cambridge.

CAMBRIDGE UNIVERSITY LIGHTWEIGHT RC. 1974. *Oarblade:* Light blue. *Singlet:* White, with university crest.

CAMBRIDGE UNIVERSITY WBC. 1895, re-established 1956, *Oarblade and Singlet:* Light blue. *Boathouse:* Trinity College Boathouse.

CENTRAL LONDON, POLYTECHNIC OF. 1965. *Oarblade:* Maroon, with vertical black, silver, black stripe. *Boathouse:* Polytechnic Boathouse, Ibis Lane, Chiswick, London W4.

CHARING CROSS HOSPITAL MEDICAL SCHOOL BC. 1977. *Oarblade:* Scarlet red, with Maltese cross and gold tip. *Singlet:* Scarlet red, with black hoop and school crest. *Boathouse:* University of London Boathouse, Hartington Road, Chiswick, London W4

CHELSEA COLLEGE. 1979.

CHERWELL BC. University Boathouse, Riverside, Oxford.

CHRIST CHURCH BC. 1832. *Oarblade:* Dark blue. *Singlet:* Dark blue. *Shorts:* Dark blue and white check.

CHRIST'S COLLEGE BC. 1830. *Oarblade:* Navy blue, tipped royal blue and white diagonally. *Singlet:* Navy blue. *Boathouse:* Victoria Bridge, Christ's College, Cambridge.

CHURCHILL COLLEGE BC. 1961. *Oarblade and Singlet:* Brown with pink stripes. *Boathouse:* St Andrew's Road, Cambridge.

CITY UNIVERSITY, THE, BC. 1966 (*formerly Northampton College BC, 1946*). *Oarblade:* Maroon, white and gold bands. *Singlet:* red. *Boathouse:* Spring Hill, Clapton, London E5.

CLARE BC. 1831. *Oarblade and Singlet:* Yellow. *Boathouse:* Cutter Ferry Lane, Clare College, Cambridge.

COLLINGWOOD COLLEGE BC. ——. *Oarblade*: Red and black with white diagonal.

CORPUS CHRISTI COLLEGE (CAMBRIDGE) BC. Ante 1830. *Oarblade:* Cherry with white bar. *Singlet:* White with cherry band. *Boathouse:* Ferry Lane, Cambridge.

CORPUS CHRISTI COLLEGE (OXFORD) BC. ——. *Oarblade:* Dark blue, two red bars. *Singlet:* Blue with pelican badge.

CORPUS CHRISTI COLLEGE WOMEN'S BC. 1977. *Oarblade:* Dark blue with two red stripes. *Singlet:* Red and dark blue.

DARWIN COLLEGE BC. *Colours:* Dark blue, with red, light blue and yellow

175

stripes. *Boathouse:* Pembroke Boathouse, Cutter Ferry Lane, Cambridge.

DOWNING COLLEGE BC. 1862. *Oarblade:* Magenta. *Singlet:* White with magenta griffon. *Boathouse:* Cutter Ferry Lane, Cambridge.

DURHAM UNIVERSITY BC. 1877. *Oarblade:* Palatinate. *Singlet:* White with diagonal palatinate stripe. *Boathouse:* River Wear, Durham.

DURHAM UNIVERSITY WBC 1982. *Oarblade:* Palatinate. *Singlet:* White with diagonal palatinate stripe. *Boathouse:* River Wear, Durham.

EAST ANGLIA, UNIVERSITY OF, BC. 1966. *Oarblade:* Light blue, with two dark blue diagonal lines. *Singlet:* Blue, with coypu emblem. *Boathouse:* Norwich RC, Whitlingham Lane, Trowse, Norwich.

EMMANUEL BC. 1824. *Oarblade:* Plain, a broad cerise bar between two narrow blue bars. *Singlet:* White, trimmed blue. *Boathouse:* Cutter Ferry Lane, Cambridge.

EXETER COLLEGE BC. 1830. *Oarblade:* Peony red. *Singlet:* Crimson. *Boathouse:* Christchurch Meadows, Oxford.

EXETER UNIVERSITY BC. 1948. *Oarblade:* Green, white spear and tip. *Singlet:* White, trimmed green. *Boathouse:* Exeter Canal. Countess Weir Swingbridge, Exeter.

FIRST AND THIRD TRINITY BC (8). 1823 (*First and Third Trinity Clubs amalgamated 1946*). *Oarblade:* Dark blue. *Singlet:* Dark blue and gold.

FITZWILLIAM COLLEGE BC. *Circa* 1884. *Oarblade:* Grey with maroon billy-goat. *Singlet:* Maroon. *Boathouse:* Via Kimberley Road, Cambridge.

GIRTON COLLEGE BC. 1980.

GOLDIE BC. ———. (*Cambridge University*). Riverside, Kimberley Road, Cambridge.

GRADUATE SOCIETY (DURHAM) BC. 1974. *Oarblade:* White. *Singlet:* White with globe.

GREY COLLEGE BC. 1960 *Oarblade:*

Red with white, black, white bar. *Singlet:* Red with white, black, white diagonal. Grey College, Durham.

GUY'S HOSPITAL BC. 1825. *Oarblade:* Navy blue, a gold bar on white. *Singlet:* White, trimmed colours. *Boathouse:* University of London, Chiswick.

HATFIELD COLLEGE BC. 1885. *Oarblade:* Navy blue, with white lion. *Singlet:* Navy blue, with white diagonal. Hatfield College, North Bailey, Durham.

HERTFORD COLLEGE BC. 1875. *Oarblade:* Maroon with two white bars. *Singlet:* Red. *Boathouse:* Tims, Long Bridges, Oxford.

HOMERTON COLLEGE BC. 1976. *Oarblade:* White, with mid-blue vertical stripe. *Singlet:* Dark blue. *Boathouse:* Riverside, Cambridge (Trinity Hall Boathouse).

HULL UNIVERSITY BC. 1947. *Oarblade and Singlet:* White with green and brown horizontal stripes. *Boathouse:* Oak Road, Hull, North Humberside.

IMPERIAL COLLEGE BC. ———. *Oarblade:* Grey, white chevron, blue and black divided tip. *Singlet:* White with grey, blue and black bands. *Boathouse:* Embankment, London SW15.

ISIS BC. ———. University Boathouse, Riverside, Oxford.

JESUS COLLEGE (CAMBRIDGE) BC. 1827. *Oarblade:* Black, two red bars. *Singlet:* Red and black. *Boathouse:* Riverside, Cambridge.

JESUS COLLEGE (OXFORD) BC. 1835. *Oarblade:* Green, white collar. *Singlet:* Green.

KEBLE COLLEGE BC. 1870. *Oarblade:* White, blue band, red chevron. *Singlet:* Dark blue with red and white diagonal.

KEELE, UNIVERSITY OF, RC. 1978. *Oarblade:* Emerald green. *Singlet:* Black with red and gold hoops. *Boathouse:* Trentham Lake, Staffs.

176

KENT, UNIVERSITY OF, RC. 1956. *Colours:* White with red and blue diagonal. *Boathouse:* The King's School Boathouse, Fordwich, Kent.

KING'S COLLEGE BC. 1858. *Oarblade and Singlet:* Purple. *Boathouse:* Logan's Way, Cambridge.

KING'S COLLEGE BC. 1837. *Oarblade:* Plain, a scarlet lion on crown. *Singlet:* Blue and white diagonal. *Boathouse:* Thames RC. London.

LADY MARGARET BC. 1825. *Oarblade and Singlet:* Scarlet. *Boathouse:* By Victoria Bridge. Cambridge.

LADY MARGARET HALL BC. 1972. *Oarblade:* Blue, with yellow/gold spear. *Singlet:* Yellow. *Boathouse:* On the Isis.

LADY SOMERSET BC. 1979. *Oarblade and Singlet:* Scarlet. *Boathouse:* By Victoria Bridge, Cambridge.

LANCASTER UNIVERSITY BC. 1964. *Oarblade:* Grey and red. *Singlet:* Red and grey. *Boathouse:* Railway Station, Halton-on-Lune.

LEEDS UNIVERSITY BC. 1919. *Oarblade and Singlet:* Green with maroon and white. *Boathouse:* Roundhay Park, Swillington Bridge, Leeds.

LEICESTER, UNIVERSITY OF, BC. 1948. *Oarblade:* White, maroon and green chevrons. *Singlet:* Maroon, white and green vertical. *Boathouse:* The Bede House, Upperton Road, Leicester.

LINACRE BC 1984. Linacre College, Oxford.

LINCOLN COLLEGE BC. 1880. *Oarblade:* Plain with light blue and dark blue collar, light blue spear. *Singlet:* Light blue, trimmed dark blue. *Boathouse:* Christchurch Meadows, Oxford.

LIVERPOOL POLYTECHNIC RC. 1977. *Oarblade:* White, with red Liver Bird. *Singlet:* Blue with horizontal amber bars and red Liver Bird, with crossed oars. *Boathouse:* Knowsley Safari Park, Knowsley, Liverpool.

LIVERPOOL UNIVERSITY BC. 1926. *Oarblade and Singlet:* White, with royal blue and sky blue band. John Cross, The Boathouse, White Man's Dam, Knowsley, Prescot, Merseyside.

LONDON HOSPITAL RC. ———. *Oarblade:* Blue with blue and white chequers. *Singlet:* White with three blue bands and griffin badge. *Boathouse:* University of London, Chiswick.

LONDON, UNIVERSITY OF, BC. ———. And University of London Tyrian Club (1963). *Oarblade:* Purple. *Singlet:* White with purple band. *Boathouse:* 81 Hartington Road, Chiswick, London W4.

LONDON, UNIVERSITY OF, WBC. ———. *Oarblade:* Purple with white tip. *Singlet:* Purple over white. *Boathouse:* University of London BC, Chiswick, London.

LOUGHBOROUGH STUDENTS RC. 1958. *Oarblade:* Maroon, with white band at tip. *Singlet:* Maroon, with single white hoop. *Boathouse:* Loughborough BC.

MAGDALENE COLLEGE BC. 1850. *Colours:* Lavender and Indigo. *Boathouse:* Victoria Bridge, Cambridge.

MAGDALEN COLLEGE BC. 1982. *Oarblade:* Black stripe on plain wood. *Singlet:* Red. *Boathouse:* River Thames, Oxford.

MANCHESTER UNIVERSITY BC. 1932. *Oarblade:* Maroon, two white chevrons. *Singlet:* Maroon, trimmed white. *Boathouse:* Dane Road, Sale (Bridgewater Canal).

MERTON COLLEGE BC. ———. *Oarblade:* White, magenta cross. *Singlet:* White or magenta.

MIDDLESEX HOSPITAL RC. 1964. *Oarblade:* Dark blue, light blue, white. *Singlet:* Blue. *Boathouse:* University of London Boathouse.

NEW COLLEGE BC. ———. *Oarblade:* Purple and yellow, vertical stripes. *Singlet:* White with purple, yellow, purple diagonals.

177

NEWCASTLE POLYTECHNIC BC. 1982. *Oarblade:* White. *Singlet:* White. *Boathouse:* North Bank, Newburn, West Swan.

NEWCASTLE UNIVERSITY BC. 1963. *Oarblade and Singlet:* White with blue star. *Boathouse:* Newburn.

NEW HALL BC. 1974. *Oarblade:* White. *Singlet:* White with black band. *Boathouse:* Fitzwilliam Boathouse.

NEWNHAM COLLEGE BC. 1896 (reformed 1973). *Oarblade:* Brown, two gold bars. *Singlet:* Brown and gold. *Boathouse:* Jesus College.

NOTTINGHAM UNIVERSITY BC. 1948. *Oarblade and Singlet:* Nottingham yellow. *Boathouse:* Trentside, West Bridgford.

ORIEL COLLEGE BC. *Circa* 1830. *Oarblade:* Dark blue, two white bars. *Singlet:* Royal blue, trimmed white. *Boathouse:* Christchurch Meadows, Oxford.

OSLER HOUSE BC. 1968 *Oarblade:* White with red staff and serpent. *Singlet:* Red. *Boathouse:* Tims, Towpath, Oxford.

OXFORD POLYTECHNIC BC. 1979. *Oarblade:* Red with black loom and spear. *Singlet:* Light blue with dark blue emblem. *Boathouse:* Falcon BC, Donnington Bridge Road, Oxford.

OXFORD UNIVERSITY BC. 1839. *Oarblade and Singlet:* Dark blue, Oxford University Boat Club, Oxford.

OXFORD UNIVERSITY HW RC. 1984.

OXFORD UNIVERSITY WBC. Re-established 1926. *Oarblade:* Oxford blue. *Singlet:* Oxford blue. *Boathouse:* Exeter College.

PEMBROKE COLLEGE (CAMBRIDGE) BC. 1832 *Oarblade:* Plain, a bar divided diagonally light and dark blue. *Singlet:* White, trimmed light blue, dark blue and martlet emblem.

PEMBROKE COLLEGE (OXFORD) BC. ———. *Oarblade:* White, cerise bar at tip. *Singlet:* Cerise and white with red rose.

PORTSMOUTH POLYTECHNIC RC. 1968. *Oarblade:* Black. *Singlet:* Black with yellow/purple hoops. *Boathouse:* Southsea RC.

QUEEN MARY COLLEGE BC. 1910. *Oarblade:* Blue with two yellow bars. *Singlet:* Blue, two yellow bands. *Boathouse:* University of London.

QUEEN'S COLLEGE, CAMBRIDGE, BC. 1830. *Oarblade:* Green, a white bar. *Singlet:* White, trimmed green.

QUEEN'S COLLEGE, THE, BC. ———. *Oarblade:* Navy blue, white horizontal stripe, white tip. *Singlet:* Navy blue with white strips. *Boathouse:* Christchurch Meadows, Oxford.

READING UNIVERSITY BC. ———. *Oarblade:* Purple and white. *Singlet:* Purple. *Boathouse:* Caversham Bridge.

READING UNIVERSITY WBC. 1939. *Oarblade:* Purple, white, a gold shell emblem. *Singlet:* Purple and white. *Boathouse:* Caversham Bridge.

RIPON AND YORK BC. ———. *Oarblade:* Brown with two gold stripes (*men*); Gold with two brown stripes (*ladies*). *Singlet:* Brown, with two gold diagonal stripes. *Boathouse:* Marygate, York.

ROBINSON COLLEGE BC. 1980. *Oarblade:* Kingfisher blue, two gold bars, white collars. *Singlet:* Royal blue, trimmed white, two gold bands (1st VIII), one gold band (2nd VIII). *Boathouse:* Jesus College Boathouse, Cambridge.

ROYAL AGRICULTURAL COLLEGE (Cirencester, Gloucestershire) BC. 1965. *Oarblade:* Maroon, black and gold bar. *Singlet:* White with black white and maroon band.

ROYAL DENTAL HOSPITAL BC. ———. *Oarblade and Singlet:* Black, purple and white. *Boathouse:* Thames RC.

ROYAL FREE HOSPITAL BC. ———. *Oarblade:* Yellow. *Singlet:* Black and yellow. *Boathouse:* University of London Boathouse.

ROYAL HOLLOWAY COLLEGE BC. 1967. *Oarblade:* Green. *Singlet:* Green with white, maroon, white diagonal. *Boathouse:* Staines BC.

ROYAL MILITARY ACADEMY SANDHURST BC. 1924 (as RMC), 1947 (as RMA). *Oarblade:* Red, with blue and gold bar, or red. *Singlet:* Red, with RMA crest. *Boathouse:* Reading School BC, Eton College BC (sculling only).

ROYAL MILITARY COLLEGE OF SCIENCE BC. ———. *Oarblade:* Light blue. *Singlet:* Royal blue.

ST AIDAN'S COLLEGE BC. 1954. *Oarblade:* Green with two white chevrons with centre maroon chevron. *Boathouse:* University College Boathouse, Prebends Bridge, Durham.

ST ANNE'S COLLEGE BC. ———. *Oarblade:* Red, with silver grey tip. *Singlet:* Red, with grey diagonal. *Boathouse:* Isis River, Oxford.

ST BARTHOLOMEW'S HOSPITAL BC. 1844. *Oarblade:* Parted palewise sable and argent, a chevron countercharged. *Singlet:* Black. *Boathouse:* University of London Boathouse.

ST CATHERINE'S COLLEGE BC. 1876. *Oarblade:* Light blue with magenta catherine wheel. *Singlet:* Light blue, trimmed magenta, with catherine wheel. *Boathouse:* Oxford University Boathouse.

ST CATHARINE'S COLLEGE CAMBRIDGE BC. ———. *Oarblade:* Claret. *Singlet:* White, trimmed claret, catherine wheel badge.

ST CHAD'S COLLEGE BC (Durham). 1904. *Oarblade:* White cross potent on olive green. *Singlet:* Green with white chevron.

ST CUTHBERT'S SOCIETY DURHAM BC.

ST EDMUND HALL BC. 1851. *Oarblade:* Plain with claret cross and claret and old gold bands at neck.

*Singlet:* Burgundy, with amber cross. *Boathouse:* Christchurch Meadows, Oxford.

ST GEORGE'S HOSPITAL BC. ———. *Oarblade:* White with red St George design. *Singlet:* Green. *Boathouse:* University of London.

ST HILD AND ST BEDE COLLEGE BC. 1976. *Oarblade:* Light blue with two dark blue chevrons. *Singlet:* Dark blue. *Boathouse:* Riverside, below College of St Hild and St Bede, Durham.

ST HILDA'S COLLEGE BC. 1980. *Oarblade:* Navy, with white triangle. *Singlet:* Navy, with white triangle across shoulder. *Boathouse:* Timms, Long Bridges, Oxford.

ST HUGH'S COLLEGE OXFORD. 1983.

ST JOHN'S COLLEGE, CAMBRIDGE. *See Lady Margaret BC.*

ST JOHN'S COLLEGE BC. ———. *Oarblade:* Saxe blue. *Singlet:* White, trimmed saxe blue. *Boathouse:* Riverside, Durham.

ST JOHN'S COLLEGE (OXFORD) BC. ———. *Oarblade:* Blue with blue cross on white shield. *Singlet:* White, trimmed blue with blue cross on shield. *Boathouse:* Christchurch Meadows, Oxford.

ST MARY'S COLLEGE DURHAM BC.

ST MARY'S HOSPITAL (MEDICAL SCHOOL) BC. ———. *Oarblade:* White, royal blue flash. *Singlet:* Royal blue with crossed oars on fleur-de-lis. *Boathouse:* University of London.

ST PETER'S COLLEGE BC. 1931. *Oarblade:* Green with yellow spear. *Singlet:* Green, trimmed yellow. *Boathouse:* Oxford University BC.

ST THOMAS'S HOSPITAL BC. 1850. *Oarblade:* Red, white and blue. *Singlet:* Trimmed blue and white. *Boathouse:* University of London.

SALFORD, UNIVERSITY OF, BC. 1965. *Colours:* Yellow and blue.

*Boathouse:* Agecroft RC.

SELWYN COLLEGE BC. 1883. *Oarblade:* White with maroon and old gold bar. *Singlet:* White with maroon and old gold hoop. *Boathouse:* Logan's Way, Cambridge.

SHEFFIELD CITY POLYTECHNIC RC. 1983. *Oarblade:* Yellow with two black diagonal stripes. *Singlet:* Yellow with two black diagonal stripes. *Boathouse:* Dam Flask Reservoir. Low Bradfield.

SHEFFIELD UNIVERSITY RC. 1965. *Singlet:* Black with two yellow diagonals. *Boathouse:* Damflask Reservoir.

SIDNEY SUSSEX BC (Cambridge). 1837. *Oarblade:* Dark blue and magenta diagonally. *Singlet:* Dark blue with magenta band.

SOUTHAMPTON UNIVERSITY BC. 1936. *Oarblade:* Plain, three maroon chevrons. *Singlet:* White with maroon, yellow and blue hoops. *Boathouse:* Oliver Road, Swaythling.

STAFF COLLEGE BC (Camberley), THE. 1980. *Oarblade:* Light blue. *Singlet:* Red.

SURREY UNIVERSITY BC. 1947. *Oarblade:* Purple and blue. *Singlet:* Purple with sky-blue band. *Boathouse:* Walton RC.

TEESSIDE POLYTECHNIC RC. 1980

TRENT POLYTECHNIC RC. 1980. *Oarblade:* Light blue, with black chevrons. *Singlet:* Black.

TREVELYAN COLLEGE, DURHAM, BC.

TRINITY COLLEGE BC. 1820. *Oarblade:* Dark blue with white bar. *Singlet:* Blue, trimmed white. *Boathouse:* Christchurch Meadow. Oxford.

TRINITY HALL BC. 1827 *Oarblade:* Black. *Singlet:* White, trimmed black. *Boathouse:* Riverside, Cambridge.

UNIVERSITY COLLEGE, DURHAM, BC. Ante 1836. *Oarblade:* Cardinal, a white chevron. *Singlet:* White, trimmed cardinal: (*80 crews*) cardinal St

Cuthbert's cross on left chest. *Boathouse:* Near the Old Mill, Prebends Bridge.

UNIVERSITY COLLEGE (OXFORD) BC. *circa* 1850. *Oarblade and Singlet:* Blue with gold cross. *Boathouse:* University Boathouse.

UNITED HOSPITALS RC

UNIVERSITY COLLEGE & HOSPITAL BC. 1920. *Oarblade:* Wedgwood blue and purple. *Singlet:* Wedgwood blue, trimmed purple. *Boathouse:* University of London Boathouse.

VAN MILDERT BC. ———. *Oarblade:* Primrose, black spear and tip. *Singlet:* White. *Boathouse:* River Wear, opposite Dunelm House.

WARWICK, UNIVERSITY OF, BC. 1966. *Oarblade:* Red with black tip and white collar. *Singlet:* White with red and black hoops. *Boathouse:* Barford-on-Avon.

WESTMINSTER HOSPITAL BC. ———. *Oarblade:* White with black portcullis. *Singlet:* White with black and grey hoops.

WINDSORIAN RC. 1984.

WOLFSON COLLEGE, CAMBRIDGE. 1983.

WOLFSON COLLEGE BC. ———. *Oarblade:* Gold, with vertical red bar. *Singlet:* Gold, with red hoop. *Boathouse:* Oxford University BC Boathouse.

WORCESTER COLLEGE BC. 1829. *Oarblade:* Pink, a black Maltese cross. *Singlet:* Black with pink Maltese cross. *Boathouse:* Christchurch Meadows, Oxford.

YORK, UNIVERSITY OF, BC. 1965. *Oarblade:* Light blue with white rose. *Singlet:* Dark blue with white rose. *Boathouse:* Fulford, York.


(*Schools*)

ABINGDON SCHOOL BC. 1840. *Oarblade:* Cerise and white. *Singlet:*

White, trimmed cerise. *Boathouse:* Wilsham Road, Abingdon.

ARCHBISHOP HOLGATE'S GS BC. 1957. *Oarblade:* Navy blue with white mitre. *Singlet:* White, trimmed royal blue with royal blue mitre badge. *Boathouse:* Scarborough Bridge, York.

AYLESTON SCHOOL, HEREFORD, BC.

BARN ELMS ROWING CENTRE. 1966. *Colours:* Light blue. *Boathouse:* Barn Elms, Putney, London SW15.

BECKET SCHOOL, THE, BC. 1949. *Oarblade:* Black, Cambridge blue, silver collar. *Singlet:* Cambridge blue. *Boathouse:* National Water Sports Centre, Holme Pierrepont.

BEDFORD SCHOOL BC. 1860. *Oarblade:* Dark blue, two white bars. *Singlet:* White with eagle in centre. *Boathouse:* The Embankment, Bedford.

BEDFORD HIGH SCHOOL RC. 1983.

BEDFORD MODERN SCHOOL BC. 1878. *Oarblade:* Black, two red bars. *Singlet:* White, with red eagle (1st 80), red or red and white (others). *Boathouse:* Bedford Schools, The Embankment, Bedford.

BEDFORDSHIRE SCHOOLS ROWING ASSOCIATION. 1979. *Oarblade:* Blue, with red, white and gold. *Singlet:* Blue. *Boathouse:* Bedford RC.

BELMONT ABBEY SCHOOL BC. 1956. *Oarblade and Singlet:* White, blue/brown. *Boathouse:* Hereford RC.

BERKHAMSTED SCHOOL BC. 1959. *Oarblade:* Oxford blue, a red gargoyle. *Singlet:* Blue and red. *Boathouse:* Newground Wharf (Grand Union Canal).

BEVERLEY SCHOOL BC. 1973. *Oarblade:* Front divided green and yellow, black back. *Singlet:* Black, with green/yellow/green hoops. *Boathouse:* 52 High Street, Kingston-on-Thames.

BRADFORD GRAMMAR SCHOOL BC. 1954. *Oarblade:* White, with maroon chevron. *Singlet:* White.

*Boathouse:* Hirst Weir, Shipley.

BRYANSTON SCHOOL BC. 1928. *Oarblade:* Plain, with dark blue and yellow bars at tip. 1st VIII blue and yellow. *Singlet:* White or navy blue, trimmed colours. *Boathouse:* On River Stour. Bryanston School, Blandford Dorset.

BRYANSTON BUFFALOES BC.

CANFORD SCHOOL BC. 1931. *Oarblade:* Garter blue, with white spear. *Singlet:* Garter blue. *Boathouse:* Canford Magna (R Stour).

CARMEL COLLEGE BC. 1954. *Oarblade and Singlet:* Purple and gold. *Boathouse:* Mongewell Park, Carmel College, Wallingford, Berks.

CHARTERHOUSE RC. 1974. *Oarblade:* Dark blue, cross stripes of maroon and pink. *Singlet:* Maroon. *Boathouse:* Shalford Road, Guildford, Surrey.

CHELTENHAM COLLEGE BC. *Ante* 1861. *Oarblade:* Red, two black chevrons. *Singlet:* White, trimmed black and red. *Boathouse:* Lower Loade, Tewkesbury.

CHISWICK SCHOOL BC. 1931. *Oarblade:* Maroon and light blue bands. *Singlet:* Maroon. *Boathouse:* Chiswick Boathouse, by Barnes Bridge.

CITY OF LONDON SCHOOL BC. ———. *Oarblade:* Black and white on maroon. *Singlet:* White. *Boathouse:* London RC, Putney.

CLIFTON COLLEGE RC. 1920. *Oarblade:* Blue, white tip and collar. *Singlet:* Blue. *Boathouse:* Clifton College, Bristol.

COKETHORPE SCHOOL BC. 1960. *Oarblade:* Silver, gold and light blue. *Singlet:* Silver. *Boathouse:* 'The Rose Revived', Newbridge.

DESBOROUGH SCHOOL RC (*formerly Maidenhead GS*). 1946. *Oarblade:* Light blue, with yellow chevron. *Singlet:* Light blue. *Boathouse:* Maidenhead RC.

DRAGON SCHOOL BC (Oxford).

DURHAM SCHOOL BC. 1847.

181

*Oarblade:* White, with green. *Singlet:* White, trimmed green. *Boathouse:* The Weir, Durham City.

DURHAM JOHNSTONE COMPREHENSIVE SCHOOL RC. 1878. *Oarblade:* White/red/blue chevron on white blade. *Singlet:* Blue. *Boathouse:* Prebends Bridge, Durham.

EALING HIGH SCHOOLS BC (*formerly Ealing Grammar School*). *1946. Oarblade:* Black, two white bars. *Singlet:* Black, trimmed white. *Boathouse:* Chiswick Boathouse, Duke's Meadows, London.

EASTBOURNE COLLEGE BC. 1928. *Oarblade:* White, with blue stag antler. *Singlet:* Dark blue. *Boathouse:* Middle Bridge, Pevensey Levels.

ELIZABETHAN BC (Westminster School).

EMANUEL SCHOOL BC. 1915. *Oarblade:* Dark blue, a gold chevron. *Singlet:* White, or dark blue and gold. *Boathouse:* Duke's Meadows, Chiswick, London W4.

ETON COLLEGE BC. 1816. *Oarblade:* The VIII – Light blue, Lower Boats – Dark blue. *Singlet:* The VIII – Light blue, Lower Boats – White, trimmed blue, green, red or brown (depending on crew). *Boathouse:* Brocas Street, Eton.

FOREST SCHOOL BC. 1952. *Oarblade:* Blue and white. *Singlet:* Blue. *Boathouse:* Spring Hill, Clapton.

FOREST SCHOOL (WINNERSH) RC. 1983. *Oarblade:* (Henley RC blades) blue with white collar. *Singlet:* Blue (yellow-white) stripes. *Boathouse:* Henley Rowing Club.

GARFORTH COMPREHENSIVE SCHOOL RC. 1972. *Oarblade:* Black, with white rose front. *Singlet:* Black. *Boathouse:* Leeds University, Swilington Bridge.

GREAT MARLOW SCHOOL BC.

HAMPTON SCHOOL BC. 1956. *Oarblade:* Black and yellow. *Singlet:* Yellow. *Boathouse:* Molesey BC.

THE HENRY MEOLES SCHOOL BC

*formerly Wallasey GS. 1922. Oarblade and Singlet:* Orange. *Boathouse:* Liverpool Victoria RC.

HEREFORD CATHEDRAL SCHOOL BC. 1883. *Oarblade:* Blue and gold chevrons. *Singlet:* Blue. *Boathouse:* Hereford RC.

HEREFORD SCHOOLS BC.

HIGH WYCOMBE ROYAL GRAMMAR SCHOOL BC. 1954 *Oarblade:* White, red, green and blue diagonals. *Singlet:* White, banded colours. *Boathouse:* Marlow RC

JUDGEMEADOW COMMUNITY COLLEGE (Leicester). 1984.

KING CHARLES I SCHOOL, KIDDERMINSTER, BC. 1960. *Oarblade:* Plain, a blue staple. *Singlet:* Black. *Boathouse:* Bewdley RC.

KING EDWARD VI SCHOOL BC. 1926. *Oarblade and Singlet:* Blue, a yellow cross. *Boathouse:* Stratford-upon-Avon BC.

KING JAMES'S COLLEGE OF HENLEY BC *formerly Henley Grammar School.* ——. *Oarblade:* Blue and yellow bands. *Singlet:* White, trimmed blue and yellow. *Boathouse:* Upper Thames RC.

KING'S COLLEGE SCHOOL BC. 1890. *Oarblade:* Navy blue and red. *Singlet:* Blue, with red hoop. *Boathouse:* Kingston RC.

KING'S SCHOOL, CANTERBURY, BC. 1890. *Oarblade:* Plain, a band of dark blue and white diagonal stripes. *Singlet:* Dark blue, trimmed white. *Boathouse:* Fordwich & Pluck's Gutter (R Stour).

KING'S SCHOOL, CHESTER, RC. 1883. *Oarblade:* Argent, two chevrons vert and azure.' *Singlet:* White. *Boathouse:* The Groves.

KING'S SCHOOL, ELY, BC. 1895. *Oarblade:* Dark blue with white bar. *Singlet:* Royal blue. *Boathouse:* Babylon, Ely.

KING'S SCHOOL, GLOUCESTER, BC. 1951. *Oarblade:* Sky or saxe blue.

*Singlet:* Sky or royal blue. *Boathouse:* Hempsted, Bristol Road (Berkeley Canal).

KING'S SCHOOL, ROCHESTER, BC. 1964. *Oarblade:* White and blue. *Singlet:* White trimmed blue. *Boathouse:* Royal Engineers RC, Maidstone.

KING'S SCHOOL, WORCESTER, BC. 1877. *Oarblade:* White, a blue spear. *Singlet:* Blue. *Boathouse:* Severn Street.

KINGSTON GRAMMAR SCHOOL BC 1889. *Oarblade:* Red, a white bar. *Singlet:* White, a red band. *Boathouse:* Aragon Avenue, Thames Ditton.

KITWOOD BOYS' SCHOOL RC. 1968. *Oarblade:* Maroon. *Singlet:* Maroon and white. *Boathouse:* Boston RC.

LADY ELEANOR HOLLES BC. 1983. *Oarblade:* Yellow/black. *Singlet:* Black, red and white, c/o Hampton School.

LADY ROHESIA, BEDFORD, BC.

LANCASTER ROYAL GRAMMAR SCHOOL BC. 1948. *Oarblade:* White, blue bar. *Singlet:* White, trimmed blue. *Boathouse:* Caton Road.

LATYMER UPPER SCHOOL BC. 1937. *Oarblade:* Light blue, with black/silver/black bands. *Singlet:* Light blue. *Boathouse:* 40a Upper School, King Street, London W6.

LONDON NAUTICAL SCHOOL. 1983 *Oarblade:* Blue. *Singlet:* Blue. *Boathouse:* Lea Rowing Club, Springhill, Clapton E5.

MAGDALEN COLLEGE SCHOOL BC. *Ante* 1870. *Oarblade:* Plain, with red/black/red bars. *Singlet:* White, with red/black/red bands. *Boathouse:* Oxford University Boathouse.

MARK RUTHERFORD SCHOOL RC. 1978. *Oarblade:* Black, with white lion of St Mark. *Singlet:* Black and White. *Boathouse:* Bedford RC.

MERCHANT TAYLOR'S SCHOOL BC. 1958 *Oarblade:* Light blue with chocolate band. *Singlet:* Light blue, with chocolate band. *Boathouse:* Field Lane, Litherland, Liverpool.

MONKTON COMBE SCHOOL BC. 1878. *Oarblade:* Blue. *Singlet:* Blue, with white hoops; white, with blue hoops (lower crews). *Boathouse:* Dundas Aqueduct, Limpley Stoke.

NEWCASTLE ROYAL GRAMMAR SCHOOL BC. 1938. *Oarblade and Singlet:* White, with black and red bands. *Boathouse:* Blaydon Royal Grammar School, Eskdale Terrace, Jesmond.

NORWICH SCHOOL BC. *Circa* 1880, refounded 1948. *Oarblade:* Dark blue with white lion. *Singlet:* White, with blue band. *Boathouse:* Whitlingham Lane, Norwich.

NOTTINGHAM BRITANNIA SCHOOLS RC. 1982. *Oarblade:* Light blue with dark blue flash. *Singlet:* Dark blue and light blue. *Boathouse:* Nottingham Britannia RC.

ORATORY SCHOOL BC. 1947. *Oarblade:* Black, with yellow and white stripes. *Boathouse:* Sheepwash Lane, Whitchurch-on-Thames.

OUNDLE SCHOOL BC. 1886. *Oarblade:* Dark blue. *Singlet:* Dark blue, or white trimmed dark blue. *Boathouse:* Tansor (R Nene).

PANGBOURNE COLLEGE BC. 1955. *Oarblade:* White, with the Devitt & Moore house flag quarterly gules and azure, a fess couped argent. *Singlet:* Quartered red and blue, with a central white rectangle (1st 80) or royal blue with red/white/red hoops.

PILGRIM SCHOOL, BEDFORD, RC.

PUTNEY HIGH SCHOOL RC.

QUEEN ELIZABETH HIGH SCHOOL BC. 1980. *Oarblade:* White, with blue and green diagonal stripes. *Singlet:* Blue, green and white. *Boathouse:* Tyne Green, Hexham.

QUEEN'S PARK HIGH SCHOOL, CHESTER, RC. ———. *Oarblade:* Red, with black tip. *Singlet:* White, red and black bands.

RADLEY COLLEGE BC. 1849.

Oarblade: Red and white. Singlet: Red (with two white hoops for 1st 80). Boathouse: Lower Radley, Abingdon, Oxon.

RATCLIFFE COLLEGE BC. 1938. Oarblade: Light blue (with royal blue, black and white chevrons for 1st 90). Singlet: (1st 80) White, trimmed colours, (others) Blue. Boathouse: Cossington Bridge, Platt's Lane, Cossington (R Soar).

READING SCHOOL BC. 1920. Oarblade: Navy blue, white collar. Singlet: Navy blue. Boathouse: Berks Bank Promenade.

READING BLUE COAT SCHOOL BC. 1947. Oarblade: Blue, a gold cross crosslet fitchy.

ST BRENDAN'S SIXTH FORM COLLEGE BC. 1965. Oarblade: Yellow, a maroon Maltese cross. Singlet: White. Boathouse: Avon County RC, Saltford.

ST EDMUND CAMPION SCHOOL BC. Oarblade: Red, white and Oxford blue. Singlet: Red, white and Oxford blue. Boathouse: City Boathouse, 1 Donnington Bridge, Oxford.

ST EDWARD'S SCHOOL BC. ———. Oarblade: Cornflower blue and gold. Singlet: Cornflower blue. Boathouse: 39 Godstow Road, Wolvercote.

ST GEORGE'S COLLEGE BC. 1957. Oarblade: Maroon, with white blocked chevron. Singlet: White, with dragon and crossed oars in maroon. Boathouse: Sunbury Lane, Walton.

ST HUGH'S COLLEGE, OXFORD, JCR BC. 1983.

ST LEONARD'S SCHOOL, DURHAM, BC. ———.

ST MARY'S COLLEGE, TWICKENHAM, BC. 1983.

ST PAUL'S SCHOOL, LONDON, BC. 1881. Oarblade: White face, black spear and tip, black back with white tip. Singlet: White, trimmed black.

ST PETER'S SCHOOL, YORK, BC. ———. Oarblade: White, with chocolate bar. Singlet: Brown, with white diagonal.

SHIPLAKE COLLEGE BC. 1963. Oarblade: Yellow and black. Singlet: Yellow, trimmed black. Boathouse: River Thames at Shiplake, Henley-on-Thames.

SHREWSBURY SCHOOL (Royal Shrewsbury School) BC. 1864. Oarblade: Dark blue, a white Maltese cross. Singlet: White, with blue trimming. Boathouse: Kingsland.

SIR JOHN DEANE'S COLLEGE BC. 1907. Oarblade: Light blue on dark blue. Singlet: Dark blue. Boathouse: Sir John Deane's Grammar School, Leftwick, Northwich, Cheshire.

SIR WILLIAM BORLASE'S SCHOOL BC. ———. Oarblade: Dark blue, a red chevron. Singlet: Dark blue. Boathouse: Marlow RC.

SOHAM VILLAGE COLLEGE RC. 1973. Oarblade: Royal blue, with old gold fleur-de-lis. Singlet: Blue. Boathouse: By Victoria Bridge, Cambridge.

SOUTH WOLDS SCHOOL, KEYWORTH, BC.

STOWE SCULLING CLUB. ———. Oarblade: White. Singlet: White, with blue and gold hoop. Boathouse: Stowe, Buckingham, Bucks.

STRODE'S COLLEGE BC. 1925. Oarblade: Plain, with green/yellow/-green bars. Singlet: Green, with yellow diagonal. Boathouse: Cooper's Close, Egham.

SUTTON SCHOOL BC. 1955. Oarblade: Maroon and white. Singlet: Maroon. Boathouse: Reading RC.

THE LEYS SCHOOL BC. 1960. Oarblade: Light blue, with dark blue and red bar. Singlet: White, trimmed colours. Boathouse: St Andrew's Road, Cambridge.

TIFFIN SCHOOL BC. 1890. Oarblade: Dark blue, two red bands. Singlet: Blue (with two red diagonals for 1st 80). Boathouse: Canbury Gardens, Kingston-on-Thames.

184

TONBRIDGE SCHOOL BC. 1891. *Oarblade:* Blue, with white boar's head. *Singlet:* Blue, with white flash. *Boathouse:* Cannon Lane, Tonbridge, Kent.

UNIVERSITY COLLEGE SCHOOL BC. 1906. *Oarblade:* Plain, with oak leaf emblem (1st 80), others maroon. *Singlet:* Maroon, with oak leaf emblem (1st 80), others maroon. *Boathouse:* Quintin BC, Chiswick.

WALLINGFORD SCHOOL BC. 1972. *Colours:* Yellow and blue

WESTMINSTER SCHOOL BC. *Ante* 1813. *Oarblade:* Pink. *Singlet:* Pink. *Boathouse:* Putney.

WIMBLEDON COLLEGE RC. 1983.

WINCHESTER COLLEGE BC. 1866. *Oarblade:* Dark blue, red chevron. *Singlet:* Red, with blue lines. *Boathouse:* On River Itchen, Domum Road.

THE WINDSOR BOYS' SCHOOL BC. 1940. *Oarblade:* Green white collar. *Singlet:* Emerald green. *Boathouse:* Barry Avenue, Windsor.

WORCESTER COLLEGE FOR THE BLIND BC. 1914. *Oarblade:* Blue stripe. *Singlet:* Blue and dark blue. *Boathouse:* Severn, Worcester.

WORCESTER ROYAL GRAMMAR SCHOOL BC. 1948. *Oarblade:* Royal blue, gold crown. *Singlet:* Myrtle green. *Boathouse:* Worcester River Sports Centre.

WYCLIFFE COLLEGE BC. 1936. *Oarblade:* Grey with red chevron. *Singlet:* Red with gold griffin and crossed oars on the left breast. *Boathouse:* Saul Junction (Berkeley Canal).

# APPENDIX II

## *The Pattern of Events*

### REGATTAS IN 1886

Aberdeen

Bala
Barnes
Bath
Bedford
Bewdley
Bradford
Bridgnorth
Brighton
Bristol
Burton-on-Trent

Cambridge
Chertsey
Chester
Chiswick
Christchurch

Dartmouth
Derby
Dover
Dullatur
Dumfries
Durham

Eastbourne
East Sheen
Eastham
Eton
Evesham

Glasgow
Gloucester
Greenock
Greenwich
Grove Park

Hammersmith
Hastings
Henley
Hereford
Hexham

Ironbridge

Kingston-upon-Thames

Lancaster
Lea
Liverpool

Loch Lomond

Maidenhead
Maidstone
Marlow
Middlesbrough
Mortlake
Moulsey (Molesey)

Newburn-on-Tyne
Northwich
Nottingham

Oxford

Port Bannatyne
Portobello
Putney

Reading
Richmond-on-Thames

St Leonards-on-Sea
Salford
Southampton
Staines
Stirling
Stourport
Stratford-upon-Avon

Talkin Tarn
Tewkesbury
Twickenham
Tynemouth

Whitby
Windsor
Worcester
Worthing

York


## REGATTAS AND OTHER OPEN EVENTS IN 1986

Aberdeen
Abingdon
Appledore

Barnes
Bath
Bedford
Berwick
Bewdley
Bewl Bridge
Bexhill
Bideford
Birmingham
Birkenhead
Boston

Bournemouth
Bradford
Brentford
Bridgnorth
Brighton
Bristol
Broxbourne
Burton-on-Trent
Burway

Cambridge
Cambois
Chester
Chiswick
Christchurch

Clapton
Coate Water, Swindon

Dartmouth
Deal
Derby
Dover
Dullatur
Dumfries
Durham

Eastbourne
Egham
Evesham
Exeter

Falmouth
Folkestone
Fowey

Glasgow
Gloucester
Gravesend
Greenock
Greenwich

Hackney
Hammersmith
Hampton
Hastings
Henley
Hereford
Herne Bay
Hexham
Hollingworth Lake
Hull
Huntingdon

Ironbridge

Kingston-upon-Thames

Lancaster
Leeds
Leicester
Loch Lomond
Loch Ore, Fife
Lochwinnoch
Loughborough
Llandaff
Lymington

Maidenhead
Maidstone
Marlow
Molesey
Monmouth
Mortlake
Mumbles

Newark
Newburn-on-Tyne
Norwich
Northampton
Northwich
Nottingham

Oxford

Paignton
Pangbourne
Penarth
Peterborough
Plymouth
Poole
Poplar
Port Bannatyne
Portobello
Putney

Reading
Richmond-on-Thames
Rochester
Ross-on-Wye
Runcorn
Ryde

St Ives
St Neots
Salford
Shanklin
Sheffield
Shrewsbury
Shoreham
South Shields
Southampton
Southsea
Staines
Stirling
Stoke-on-Trent
Stockton
Stourport

Stratford-upon-Avon
Strathclyde
Sudbury
Swanage

Talkin Tarn
Thames Ditton
Thorpe Park
Torquay
Totnes
Twickenham
Tynemouth

Wallingford
Walton-on-Thames
Weybridge
Whitby
Wimbleball Lake
Worcester
Worthing

York

## 1986 Regattas Calendar

| Month | Thames and South East | North West, W. Midlands, WAGS and Wessex | Northern, Yorks & H'side, E. Midlands and Eastern | Coast, W of England and Hants & Dorset | Welsh ARA | Scottish ARA |
|---|---|---|---|---|---|---|
| Feb | Marlow Fours Head | Stourport Head | | University Head | | Stirling Marathon |
| | Hampton Head | WMRC Invitation Training Head | Head of the Nene (Peterborough) | | | |
| | Abingdon Small Boats Head | | | | | |
| | Henley Fours Head | Gloucester Head | Norwich Head | | | Glasgow Charities (Invitation) |
| | Greenwich Head | | | | | Aberdeen Head |
| | Burway Head | | Wear Head | | | |
| | Watney Scullers Head | | Trent Head | | | |
| Mar | Molesey Veterans Head | Worcester Head | | | | Scottish Schools Fours Head |
| | Henley Schools Head | Runcorn Eights Head | | | | Dumfries Octo-Centenary Eights Head (Invitation) |

| Month | Thames and South East | North West, W. Midlands, WAGS and Wessex | Northern, Yorks & H'side, E. Midlands and Eastern | Coast, W of England and Hants & Dorset | Welsh ARA | Scottish ARA |
|---|---|---|---|---|---|---|
| | Head of the Medway (Fours) | | | | | |
| | Reading University Head | Avon County Schools Head | Yorkshire Head | | | Clydesdale Fours Head |
| | Women's Eights Head | | Tyne Head | | | |
| | Sons of the Thames Small Boats Head | | Bedford Eights Head | | Welsh Head | |
| | Schools Head | | | | | |
| | Kingston Head | North of England Head (Chester) | | | | Glasgow RC Eights Head |
| | | | Broxbourne Scullers Head | Head of the Ouse | | |
| | Head of the River | | | | | |
| | Vesta Veterans Head | | | | Welsh Scullers Head | Glasgow RC LD Sculls |
| | University Boat Race | Northwich Head | | | | |
| Apr | Scullers Head | | | | | Clydesdale |
| | | | Bedford Small Boats Head | Fowey Head | | |
| | Reading Sprint | | Hackney Boro & Lea Junior | Head of the Plym | | |
| | | | Head of the Cam | | | |
| | Hammersmith | Chester Veterans & Juniors | Eastern Region | Southampton Head | | Clyde ARC |
| | | Runcorn | | Bewl Bridge Coastal | | |

| Month | Thames and South East | North West, W. Midlands, WAGS and Wessex | Northern, Yorks & H'side, E. Midlands and Eastern | Coast, W of England and Hants & Dorset | Welsh ARA | Scottish ARA |
|---|---|---|---|---|---|---|
| May | Putney Amateur | Evesham | Playboat | Head of the Dart | | Castle Semple |
| | Bourne Women's (Mortlake) | Merseyside | Leicester | | | |
| | Metropolitan | | York Spring | | | Edinburgh UBC Sprint |
| | | Evesham Sprint | Norwich | | | |
| | | | Bedford Schools | | | Aberdeen |
| | Wallingford | Sefton Sprint | Sheffield | | | |
| | | Avon County Schools | Tynemouth | | | |
| | Mortlake Spring | Shrewsbury | Derby City | | | |
| | | | Tyne at Home | | | Strathclyde Park |
| | | Shrewsbury Sprint | Cambridge | | | |
| | Thames Ditton | | Derby City Sprint | | | |
| | Curlew | Hereford Schools & Junior | Tyne | | | |
| | Putney Town | | Cambridge Sprint | | | |
| | Walton Junior | | Nottingham City | | | |
| | Vesta Dashes | | Durham City | | | |
| | Chiswick | Worcester | Bradford | Seaford | | Glasgow RC |
| | | Chester | Nottingham City | Shanklin | | |
| | | Northwich Sprint | Hexham | Ryde | Monmouth | |
| | Kingston Sprint | Hereford | | | | |
| | | Northwich | | | | |
| | Twickenham | Coate | Nottingham International | Folkestone | | |
| | | Birmingham | | Shanklin | | |

| Month | Thames and South East | North West, W. Midlands, WAGS and Wessex | Northern, Yorks & H'side, E. Midlands and Eastern | Coast, W of England and Hants & Dorset | Welsh ARA | Scottish ARA |
|---|---|---|---|---|---|---|
| June | Walton<br>Women's Summer | Hollingworth Lake | Wansbeck<br>Nottingham International<br>Boston Town Sprint<br>National Schools<br>Stockton | Plymouth<br>Brighton | | |
| | Bewl Bridge | | Peterborough<br>Loughborough & National Veterans<br>Peterborough Sprint | | | |
| | Reading Amateur<br>Barnes & Mortlake | Bridgnorth<br>Lymington<br>Agecroft<br>Wessex Youth Afloat | Bedford Ladies & Star<br>Durham | Worthing<br>Southampton | | Scottish Senior Junior & Schools Championships |
| June | Marlow<br>Horseferry | Stratford upon Avon | Star Sprint<br>York Summer | Milford on Sea | | |
| | Richmond<br>Reading Town<br>Weybridge Ladies | Lancaster<br>Ironbridge | Northampton<br>Leeds | Herne Bay<br>Hasting Coalporters<br>Bexhill | | Dumfries Octo-Centenary |
| July | Greenwich<br>Henley Royal | Ironbridge Sprint | Newark | Poole | | |
| | Kingston<br>Egham | | Huntingdon<br>Talkin Tarn<br>Rother Valley<br>Bedford<br>Burton | Exeter<br>Southsea | Llandaff | |

| Month | Thames and South East | North West, W. Midlands, WAGS and Wessex | Northern, Yorks & H'side, E. Midlands and Eastern | Coast, W of England and Hants & Dorset | Welsh ARA | Scottish ARA |
|---|---|---|---|---|---|---|
| | Molesey | Evesham Ladies | Bedford Quarts Sprint | Totnes | Mumbles | Port Bannatyne |
| | | | National Championships Sudbury | | | |
| | Staines | Bewdley | | Deal | Cleddau | Commonwealth Games |
| | Henley Town & Visitors | Bewdley Sprint | St Neots | Swanage | | |
| | Upper Thames Sprint | | St Neots Sprint | Shoreham | | |
| | Maidenhead | Stourport | | Bournemouth | | |
| | | | | Wimbleball | | SARA Jollyboat Championships |
| | | | St Ives | Dover | | |
| | | Stourport Sprint | | Woolston | | |
| | Oxford City | | | Paignton | | |
| Aug | Abingdon Sprint | | World Championships | Appledore | | |
| | | | | Christchurch | | |
| | Danson Dashes | Gloucester | | BTC (Southampton) | | |
| | | | | Torquay | | |
| | | | | Eastbourne | | |
| | Trafalgar | Bristol Avon | | Dartmouth | Penarth | |
| | | Ross on Wye | | | | |
| | | Trentham | | | | |
| | Poplar & Blackwall | Trentham Sprint | | | | Glasgow RC Sprint |

| Month | Thames and South East | North West, W. Midlands, WAGS and Wessex | Northern, Yorks & H'side, E. Midlands and Eastern | Coast, W of England and Hants & Dorset | Welsh ARA | Scottish ARA |
|---|---|---|---|---|---|---|
| Sep | Gravesend Sprint<br>Hammersmith Boro & Autumn | Worcester Veteran & Junior | Tees<br>Newt Sprint<br>Cambridge Autumn<br>Talkin Tarn Veteran<br>Lea Autumn<br>Sheffield Sprint<br>Bradford Autumn<br>Tyne Sprint<br>Norfolk Sculls<br>Boston Marathon<br>York Sprint<br>Peterborough Autumn | Bideford<br>Bideford (Invitation) | | Castle Semple Sprint<br>Clydesdale Sprint<br>Nithsdale Sprint<br>St Andrews Sprint |
| | Pairs Head | Chester LD Sculls | | | | |
| Oct | Wallingford Sculls<br>Rochester Head<br>Reading Sculls<br>Reading Fours<br>Maidstone Scullers Head<br>Weybridge Sculls<br>Curlew Head<br>Marlow Sculls<br>Upper Thames Fours & Small Boats Head | Grosvenor Women's<br>Worcester Small Boats Head<br>Runcorn October Head<br>Dee Autumn Head | Hylton LD Sculls<br>St Ives Small Boats Head<br>Ancholme Head<br>Wansbeck LD Sculls<br>Cambridge Autumn Fours | | Welsh Autumn Scullers Head | Clyde ARC Sprint<br>Clydesdale Scullers Head |

| Month | Thames and South East | North West, W. Midlands, WAGS and Wessex | Northern, Yorks & H'side, E. Midlands and Eastern | Coast, W of England and Hants & Dorset | Welsh ARA | Scottish ARA |
|---|---|---|---|---|---|---|
| Nov | Henley Sculls<br>Watney Fours<br>Pangbourne Junior Sculls<br>Fours Head<br>Kingston Small Boats Head<br>Head of the Bewl<br>Hampton Junior Small Boats Head<br>Vesta Winter & Veterans<br>Tiffin Sculls | Shrewsbury Head<br>Monkton Bluefriars Head<br>Chester Small Boats Head<br>Evesham Head | Nottingham Small Boats Head<br>Bedford Autumn Small Boats Head<br>Boston Small Boats Head<br>Tees LD Sculls<br>Newark Small Boats Head<br>Tyne LD Sculls<br>Cambridge Small Boats Head<br>Great Ouse Marathon<br>Hull Small Boats Head<br>Wansbeck Fours Head<br>York Small Boats Head | | Monmouth Small Boats Head | Glasgow RC Fours Head |
| Dec | Walton Small Boats Head<br>Burway Small Boats | Wycliffe Head<br>Head of the Float (Liverpool) | Hull Fours Head<br>Rutherford Head | | | |

# Index

198

199